P9-EAO-708

BUILD YOUR OWN

OUTDOOR STRUCTURES

■ IN BRICK ■

BUILD YOUR OWN
OUTDOOR STRUCTURES
■ IN BRICK ■

PENNY SWIFT & JANEK SZYMANOWSKI

Riverside Community College
Library
4800 Magnolia Avenue
Riverside, CA 92506

TH 4961 .S9497 1997

Swift, Penny.

Build your own outdoor
structures in brick

A book of this nature takes time to produce, and there are always a huge number of people to thank when production is complete. Some provide us with locations to photograph, others assist us with the projects. Professionals in various fields also offer advice and share their expertise. We cannot note them all in print, but our gratitude goes to everyone.

This particular title has relied to a large extent on practical information and step-by-step photographs, as well as plans and pictures aimed at inspiring the reader.

Even though we have drawn information from numerous quarters, one company stands out, and a very special thank you must go to Corobrik, manufacturers of clay bricks and maxi-blocks. In particular, we owe our gratitude to Mike Ingram, one of the company's regional directors, who not only organized the projects, but also took time off on weekends to pose for the step-by-step photographs. His enthusiasm and willingness to advise when off duty was inspiring and has undoubtedly helped to make this book a reality.

Several consultants on various continents read the manuscript to ensure international accuracy. We thank them all, but especially Steve Crosswell, regional director of the Portland Cement Institute, and once again, Mike Ingram. It is a challenge to write a book which will appeal to, and relate to, people in so many different regions. These are some of the experts who have made it possible. Thank you.

Finally, we would like to acknowledge the assistance of the publishing team in producing this book.

First published in the UK in 1997 by
New Holland (Publishers) Ltd
London • Cape Town • Sydney • Singapore

Reprinted 1997

24 Nutford Place, London W1H 6DQ, UK
PO Box 1144, Cape Town 8000, South Africa
3/2 Aquatic Drive, Frenchs Forest, NSW 2086, Australia

Distributed by Sterling Publishing Company, Inc
387 Park Avenue South, New York, NY 10016

Distributed in Canada by Sterling Publishing
C/o Canadian Manda Group, One Atlantic Avenue, Suite 105,
Toronto, Ontario, Canada M6K 3E7

Copyright © in text Penny Swift 1997
Copyright © in photographs Janek Szymanowski 1997
Copyright © in published edition New Holland (Publishers) Ltd 1997

Editors Richard Pooler and Elizé Lübbe
Designers Dean Pollard and Gaelyn Quixley
Cover design Dean Pollard and Gaelyn Quixley
Design assistant Lellyn Creamer
Ilustrator Janek Szymanowski
U.S. adaptation: Josephine Bacon, American Pie, UK

Reproduction by cmyk Prepress, Cape Town
Printed and bound by Tien Wah Press (Pte) Ltd, Singapore

ISBN 1 85368 679 4 (hb)
ISBN 1 85368 741 3 (pb)

All rights reserved. No part of this publication may be reproduced, stored in a retrieval system, or transmitted in any form or by any means, electronic, mechanical, recording, photocopying or otherwise, without the written permission of the copyright owners.
The information in this book is true and complete to the best of our knowledge. All recommendations are made without guarantee on the part of the authors and the publishers. The authors and publishers disclaim any liability for damages or injury resulting from the use of this information.

CONTENTS

Anyone who values an outdoor lifestyle will appreciate a well-designed garden which incorporates functional areas for entertaining, relaxing, or simply sitting outside.

This does not mean that you need a large spread. Even a small area may be planned to meet the needs of a family that enjoys outdoor living. What you do need, though, are some permanent structures which will facilitate your lifestyle. Built-in seating, tables, and barbecue structures will encourage people to spend time outdoors in fine weather. A pergola or gazebo will create shelter, a sandpit will provide a place for little children to play, and raised planters, ponds, pools, and fountains will all add charm and character to the outdoor space.

While many garden structures are decorative, many more are strictly utilitarian. Simple box-shaped designs, topped with a weatherproof lid, may be used to store firewood, coal, or even folding outdoor furniture. A three-sided enclosure built adjacent to a wall may house garbage cans, and similar arrangements may be used to make compost, provided the design allows sufficient air to enter the walls.

A pond or fountain may be included in the design of a wall, while steps frequently feature planters on either side. Permanent seating is a welcome addition to any patio.

There are various materials which may be chosen to construct these features, but masonry is undoubtedly the most common, as well as the most durable. Almost all of the surviving structures from the ancient world were made from masonry units of some kind, and many of those structures which have disappeared were either destroyed by warfare or demolished by man. Masonry is eminently suitable for all the structures mentioned here. Not only will it last well, but it requires relatively little maintenance.

Although the focus of this book is on brickwork, masonry structures take many forms, depending on how a specific type of building is used.

Clay bricks (including adobe mud blocks) are amongst the oldest and most universal materials available. In ancient times, they were simply left in the sun to dry. Nowadays, most clay bricks are fired in huge kilns to extremely high temperatures which make them hardy and ideal for all types of building work. Size, color, and finish vary from place to place. They can be used in any climatic conditions, and are available all over the world.

Concrete bricks and blocks are a more recent invention, and one which is generally less expensive than clay. Although concrete bricks, molded to roughly the same size and shape as clay bricks, are solid, the larger blocks are hollow. This makes them easy to work with and simple to reinforce.

Another option is reconstituted or reconstructed stone, also made from concrete (see page 25), but molded in imitation of natural stone. Not only is this material uniform in size (unlike stone), making it fine for the do-it-yourself builder, but it is also generally less expensive than the real thing. Of course stone, which is classified as masonry, is perfect for garden structures, and the basic techniques and skills required for bricklaying may be adapted to stonework.

Many people who have never worked with bricks and mortar find the prospect daunting, but the skills and techniques involved are really not hard to pick up. Learning them takes time and patience, but once you have mastered them, you are sure to find many ways of utilizing your new-found abilities to add to and further improve your outdoor environment.

This book will help you understand what is involved, illustrating in a clear, visual manner the skills you will need to master for particular projects. At the same time, it will help you to decide which tasks may be undertaken by

Simple brick pillars form the basic framework for a charming, shady arbor.

others who may be more competent in certain areas. For instance, you may be more than happy to undertake the physical construction work yourself, but unsure of the technicalities of drawing the plans. If you are unfit, you may prefer to hire laborers to do the more arduous tasks (for instance mixing concrete and mortar) while you tackle those jobs which require a little more expertise. Alternatively (and this is a real option for many people), you may feel your talents lie in organizing a team of subcontractors and laborers who will do everything for you. Even members of your family may be prepared to help! But you will still want to be involved in the planning stages of the project, and will benefit from the many suggestions and ideas offered here.

Most of the possibilities given within the pages of this book are minor building projects, but there are still many potential pitfalls and possible obstacles which every home handyman should try to avoid. Not only can these threaten to delay the building program, but they may also add unnecessary costs. Of course, most problems can be avoided with proper planning and a thorough understanding of what is involved. To achieve a professional finish, you should also take a logical approach and follow the project through systematically.

Build Your Own Outdoor Structures in Brick is designed to help you to complete your project successfully, regardless of the specific route you plan to take, and irrespective of how much of the physical work you intend doing yourself. Introductory sections explain basic planning skills and will help you decide what your needs and priorities are, and how to accommodate them. A variety of suitable sites are suggested, along with guidelines that should enable you to establish which is the right location for your own brick structure. Since cost is invariably a vital factor, we suggest ways in which you can cut down on expenditure. There is also information about the various professionals who

Brick has been used to build planters, a garden seat, and a simple barbecue unit.

may be able to help you in certain areas, and a useful section which examines the kinds of regulations and building codes which may affect your particular project.

A host of design ideas is provided and explained in layman's terms, enabling anyone to create an attractive feature which blends with their existing outdoor environment. The importance of using compatible materials is highlighted, and the relevance of harmony and balance, along with the significance of size and proportion, are considered in a straightforward manner. A breakdown of the possibilities which may be explored when using bricks and blocks of various kinds is given, and a range of style options is recommended. Since even a simple brick pergola or gazebo may incorporate a roof of some sort, numerous suitable roofing materials are assessed, as is a comprehensive range of masonry building units.

For those wanting to tackle more complicated projects, there is some

basic information on extensions and additions, as well as a detailed look at what is involved in creating an outdoor kitchen or a barbecue. Traditional garden structures, including plant houses and utility structures, are also discussed.

The full spectrum of tools and materials required for bricklaying is itemized and some helpful hints given regarding how to assess quantities correctly. Although the emphasis in this book is obviously on brickwork, the preparation and use of concrete, which is essential for foundations, is also discussed briefly. Basic building methods, essential principles of construction, and the best techniques are then explained.

In a separate step-by-step section, these building methods are illustrated succinctly in photographic form. The aim here is not to follow through one project as such, but to present a hands-on sample of the techniques which you will need to tackle the range of plans presented on pages 52–61.

Any project which involves the construction of a permanent feature must be well planned. If it is not, you are likely to waste time and money. You should assess your needs carefully and consider exactly what function your brick structure is to fulfill. You can then decide exactly where to site the feature and establish how much assistance will be required. Before you go any further, you will also need to cost the project and ensure that you are able to fund it fully. It pays to plan properly right from the start. If you are systematic and thorough, the entire project should run smoothly and you will be proud of the end result.

YOUR NEEDS

Every homeowner's needs are different, and only you can decide what will suit your own and your family's circumstances.

A major element to consider at the outset is your lifestyle. If you entertain frequently and favor the alfresco approach in good weather, you will probably need a fairly elaborate arrangement which might even include an outdoor kitchen with storage areas. Seating and built-in tables are also options worth considering. Perhaps you and your family spend as much time as possible outdoors, soaking up the sun and enjoying the fresh air. In addition to the practical functions of seating and cooking facilities, you may also want to consider decorative features like planters and ponds which will improve the general appearance of a patio or courtyard. Of course, a permanent masonry structure will be part of the general garden design, but it must be planned with your needs in mind, even if you decide to employ a professional to devise an outdoor scheme for you.

If you are an indoor person, but your living room overlooks a spot which will benefit from similarly ornamental features, your needs will be slightly different. For instance, you may love the sound of trickling water, in which case a fountain should be positioned so that it can be both seen and heard from inside the house.

Your children may spend more time outdoors than you do, and a little-used patio could become a favorite play area if given the benefit of a plant-covered pergola for shade. You could perhaps build a brick-sided sandpit at one end for toddlers, or a simple lean-to, comprising a low wall which supports roof sheeting, to provide an all-weather play shelter for older children. This could even become a storage facility for bicycles and other recreational items.

In the garden itself, you may want features such as planters, steps, raised ponds, and walled flower beds, depending on the layout of the area. Pergolas and solid brick arches may also be required as a part of the general design.

Do not forget to consider the utility areas, especially if you want to hide garbage cans or if you like to pack compost into a neat enclosure.

Finally, think about any immediate needs which may change. Make absolutely certain you can adapt the plan to accommodate change.

CHOOSING THE RIGHT SITE

Brick structures, however low or small, cannot be moved, so it is essential to make certain that they are sited correctly. Mistakes can be expensive – if not impossible – to rectify.

The type of feature or structure you are planning to build will largely determine where it is to be located. Built-in benches, for instance, will usually be used to their full potential if constructed on a patio. Presuming that you have an established patio, or have pinpointed an area where you plan to build one, you will need to determine exactly where to place the seating. Ideally it should be reasonably sheltered from prevailing winds, and positioned to take advantage of a view, either beyond the garden or within its confines. However, you may want seating away from the house. Perhaps

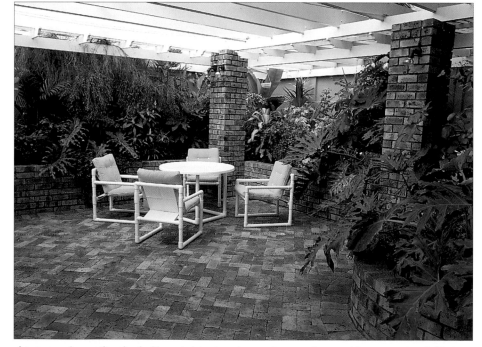

An expansive patio, shaded by a brick-piered pergola, may be used for several activities.

in a rose or herb garden, or alongside a trickling stream (if you are lucky enough to have one meandering through your garden.)

Similarly, a structure intended for outdoor cooking will normally be sited on a patio – more often than not, quite close to the house. Alternatively, you can build it up against a boundary wall which screens the site from the wind, or alongside an outbuilding which offers storage space.

The most sensible approach is to scrutinize every possible location and then examine the advantages and disadvantages of each. Make a list and note down your preferences in relation to the function of the structure and your needs.

If you are starting from scratch, sit down with a piece of paper and a pencil, and sketch some ideas. It is preferable to use graph paper to help you work to scale. Mark all the established features and buildings, trees, large rocks, and even shrubs which you want to retain. Then draw in the basic framework of walls, hedges, paths, and patios, and identify any definable activity centers (a utility area for washing lines, a vegetable or herb garden, an entertainment patio, play area, and so on). Note the direction of prevailing winds and spots which get more than average sun or shade.

Accessibility

An important factor for almost any structure in the garden is accessibility which will, to a large degree, determine its usefulness. If you cannot get to a raised planter with ease, you will tend to neglect the plants and flowers growing in it; if you have to push through shrubbery to reach a seat, there is little point in having it there, even if it has been built to capture a great view. If a masonry gazebo can only be reached by climbing a steep flight of steps, its usefulness will be limited to that of a hideaway only for those who are healthy enough to make the ascent!

Visibility

Obviously, a decorative feature must be sited where it can be seen to best

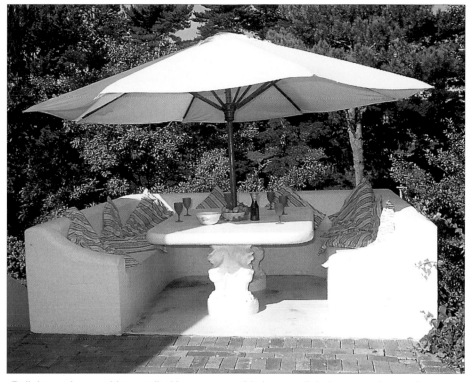

Built-in seating combines well with a precast table in a small, intimate outdoor eating area.

A two-tiered pond built out of facebrick is an ideal design for a sloping garden.

During the planning phase, before any major decisions are made and money is spent, it is essential to check legalities with your local architectural committee or building department. Many will require plans and specifications for any masonry structure, and there may be limitations in terms of what and where you may build.

If you go ahead without the necessary approval, you could find yourself having to demolish the fruits of your labor. Furthermore, there may be other penalties such as a hefty fine.

Remember that a primary motivation for establishing these codes and regulations relates to safety. Your local zoning board wants to be sure that structures are sound and will not collapse.

Although specific requirements and details vary enormously from state to state, it is possible to generalize in terms of the type of standards set nationwide. Many of these relate to what may simply be considered "good building practice."

You will find that there are various minimum requirements relating to foundations, the height of various structures, drainage, and so on. There are also minimum specifications regarding materials (particularly when these are structural elements), while other rules relate to boundaries, building lines, and certain zoning laws.

Of course, not all of these relate to garden brickwork. but it is vital to find out which codes and regulations will affect you. If your area is prone to earthquakes this is an important factor in how brickwork is used.

If you are required to present working drawings, you will probably have to submit a site plan indicating boundaries, building lines, existing buildings, and any major feature like a swimming pool or shed, all clearly shown in relation to the existing structures. Proposed new work will usually be colored on the plan. These colors are specific and must relate to the

materials which are to be used (masonry, timber, concrete, and so on). You may also have to indicate the contours of the site, as well as present sections and elevations to illustrate the proposed structure. Drainage installations may also have to be shown, along with any structures you wish to demolish.

If you plan to build on a boundary, it may be necessary to get written consent from your neighbors before your proposals can be considered by the authorities. If a building permit is required, you will need to pay any fees or dues before work can begin.

Most planning boards and committees will provide a checklist of what is required. An architect or draftsman will be familiar with these criteria.. If your house is old and you do not have the plans, consult the relevant authorities before employing somebody to draw these up from scratch. The originals will most likely be on file and you will be able to obtain copies.

Most local boards require plans and an outline of specifications for any brick structures to be constructed in the garden.

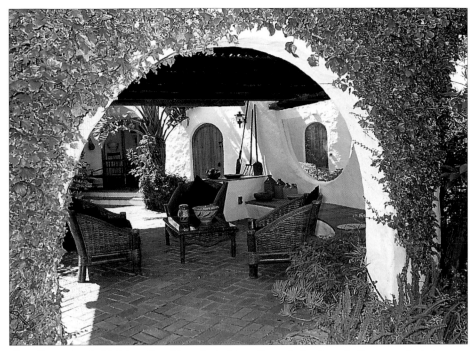

A well-constructed brick patio with walled sides offers shelter from both sun and wind.

advantage. A strictly utilitarian structure, on the other hand, should be positioned out of view.

If you are building something which is practical, but will be located on a patio or near to an entrance, you will need to ensure that it is also an attractive feature. A barbecue is a good example, as frequent use tends to blacken the walls and it can become an eyesore. Siting it away from the house can be inconvenient, and even if it is linked to a patio, the cook may be left to do the hard labor alone. A little camouflage, with potted plants, clay ornaments, and other weather-proof items could save the day.

Conditions
The microclimate of your garden is another important factor to consider. Prevailing winds are an obvious consideration when siting built-in benches and other alfresco eating and cooking structures. It is preferable to chose a sheltered spot, and one that will not become damp and cold – you will want to get the maximum possible use from these features.

Planters should also be reasonably protected from wind and, in hot climates, from the sun as well. Take full advantage of existing walls and screens and note the spots where trees provide natural shelter.

COST
Cost is a factor that cannot be ignored, and can put a damper on any project. With careful planning and conscientious budgeting, though, you can keep costs reasonable and wastage to a minimum. The first step is to establish what kind of outlay you will have to make to be able to build the features you are planning. Try to be as accurate as possible. Avoid guesswork for even the most minor projects and gather as much information as you can.

If you already have plans, you should be able to quantify the materials required relatively easily. Otherwise, sketch the proposed structure to scale and then work out what you will need, following the guidelines given on pages 32–37.

You will need to estimate the total area of all the brickwork, which will give an indication of the number of bricks needed. If the structure is to be rendered, the area will also determine how much cement, lime, and sand will be required. The number of bricks determines quantities of cement, lime, and sand for bricklaying. You will then need to calculate what you need for the concrete foundation (see page 37).

Since there is always some wastage (bricks get broken and sand blows away), so you should order slightly

A raised pond has been sited in the center of a courtyard to create a focal point.

Paving can be laid by the amateur, but larger structures may require professional help.

contractor, or even a bricklayer, may be the person whose help you require. Otherwise you may just want to employ a laborer to help you.

Before you employ people, find out what their qualifications are, check that they are properly licensed (where applicable), and ask to see examples of their work. If possible, visit some of the sites on which they have worked and talk to the owners. Also establish exactly how they plan to go about the job. If, for instance, you are hiring someone to undertake the entire operation, check whether this person plans to subcontract a portion of the job (the actual construction, for instance). In such a case it may be less expensive to consider doing the job a different way.

more of each material than you think you will need. Do not forget to add the extra amount to the initial costings. Order about 5–10% more than you have calculated. If additional materials are to be used, for instance for roofing or storage areas, these must also be costed, along with any labor you are planning to employ. Professional fees (if any) should also be included.

All sorts of items can increase the costs, but if you know exactly what is required, you can budget accordingly. You may even be able to stagger the project and complete it as additional funds become available.

PROFESSIONAL ASSISTANCE

Unless you have some kind of building experience, there is a good chance you will need the assistance of at least one professional. Since plans are often required for masonry structures, the person who is most likely to draw these up will be a draftsman or architect who can formalize your ideas on paper and ensure that they are acceptable to the authorities in your area. If the features you are planning are part of an integrated landscape scheme, you may decide to use the services of a landscape architect. If you feel you cannot tackle the building work yourself, a building

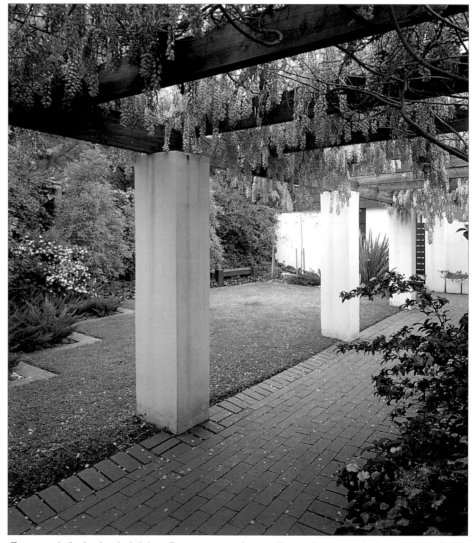

Even a relatively simple brick walkway or pergola usually requires plans before you can build.

Architect and architectural designer

An advantage of employing an architect or designer to tackle garden brickwork projects is that he or she has been trained in building styles, and will be able to create an effect which blends with the existing house and outbuildings on your property. Often a short consultation is all that is required and you can then approach a draftsman (see below) to draw up any required plans. Architects will usually tackle this type of project only if they were involved with the initial design of the house. It is usually a better idea to consult a landscape architect who specializes in gardens and other outdoor areas.

Landscape architect and landscaper

The types of brick structure considered here are very much a part of garden design and landscaping as a whole. It is therefore advisable to seek the services of somebody who specializes in this field. Bear in mind that a landscape architect has a professional qualification, while many "landscapers" may simply be garden specialists with varying amounts of knowledge and experience rather than formal training. The person you decide to use will depend on your needs and the abilities and expertise of the professionals available in your area.

Draftsman

Architects and designers frequently subcontract draftsmen to draw up their plans for them. If you know what you want, you could contact one directly to do the same for you. Most draftsmen have a working knowledge of the materials required as well as the local zoning requirements. Make sure that you approach the right person before you go ahead and spend money on plans.

Building contractor

Many builders will agree to undertake garden brickwork projects, but not all of them are competent. Make absolutely certain you have reliable recommendations and inspect work completed by the builder you plan to

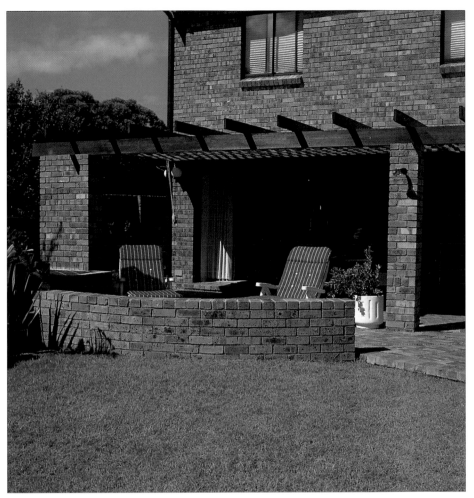

A brick pergola and adjoining wall have been designed to match the style of the house.

use. Also check that he is in a position to submit plans on your behalf (if these are required.) If he is not, the chances are that he is simply subcontracting labor and does not have an established business. Before signing any agreements, confirm whether the building contractor will provide all the materials. If you are able to source less expensive materials you might cut costs by fixing a labor-only contract.

Some building companies specialize in specific types of structure, including pergolas, carports, gazebos, and barbecues. If any of these features fits into your design scheme, you may want to get quotations from the companies offering them. Again, it is wise to check how much of the project will be completed by the contractor himself , and to compare this quotation with the cost of doing the job yourself or doing your own sub-contracting.

Subcontracting

A number of skilled workers, including bricklayers and stonemasons, may be hired for the job. Most will charge an hourly rate, although you may be able to set a payment for the entire project. You will have to supervise the work yourself and it is therefore essential that you have a basic understanding of all the procedures involved.

Locating competent subcontractors can be difficult, although you can often rely on referrals from friends or neighbors who have recently had building work done. Alternatively, check the classifieds in your local newspaper or the Yellow Pages, but don't forget to ask for references.

It is a good idea to check the legal implications of hiring casual labor. You may need to observe certain labor regulations, as well as health and safety regulations, and Workers' Compensation insurance.

A trim brick plinth beneath a garden lamp.

Good design is an essential element of any garden scheme. Not only must the brick structures you are planning blend with the architectural style and finish of your house, but they must also suit the garden environment in which they are to be located. It is important that larger features do not block sunlight or spoil a vista, and that nothing looks as though it were an afterthought which was built in a rush.

There are so many design options for masonry structures that it can be confusing to those without experience. But if you follow a few basic rules, and rely on common sense, you will find that it is really not that difficult to create something which is both practical and visually pleasing.

If you get stuck, reconsider the possibility of seeking professional guidance at this early stage.

DESIGN BASICS

An excellent starting point is to consider the garden as an extension of your home. Not only will this give you an idea of suitable materials for garden buildings, features, and small structures of all types, but it will also guide you in terms of size, scale, and proportion. It may even suggest a suitable style for your structure.

The kind of garden you have serves as a guide. If it is essentially formal, with straight lines and clearly defined beds, the brickwork should also be formal. An informal garden with curved

A low brick planter alongside the house has been rendered to match the walls of the building.

paths, natural rockeries, and island beds will benefit from a less austere approach. Seating may be curved, or simply interspersed with planters to create a more harmonious effect, and ponds built in an irregular shape. The design of a structure which features straight lines and square corners (and by the very nature of brickwork, many do) may be softened by planting or placing pots on or around it.

Balance and proportion

A variety of elements are found in outdoor areas, big and small. These range from trees, shrubs, and flowers, to the vast array of structures which may be built from masonry. One of the fundamental principles of good design is that balance is created between all of these components. Furthermore, they must be combined so that there is harmony between what nature provides and what we are able to construct ourselves.

If there is too much brickwork and it is not softened by plants, it will tend to look out of place, incongruous, and unbalanced. If any structure is not in proportion to the garden (or patio) and the house, it will look discordant; if it is simply too large, and out of proportion, it will be too dominant and will ruin the whole effect.

Contrast

Contrast is another fundamental requirement within the garden, but it should not be obtrusive or obvious. Instead, it should be used to introduce a kind of pattern and texture. There are various ways of achieving this, but one of the most obvious is to combine hard elements (including brickwork) with soft landscaping or planting. Not only are the walls of a structure juxtaposed with natural elements found outdoors, but they can be softened further by planting along the base, or by the addition of built-in containers as part of the design.

Various structures will introduce shadows into the garden, and this, in itself, is a form of contrast. For instance, the beams of a pergola will create a pattern of straight lines across

Built-in brick furniture should be in proportion to the size of the patio area.

An unusual facebrick mailbox matches the style of other brick structures in the garden.

the ground when the sun shines, while a series of archways will introduce an uneven play of light and shade.

Color, too, can create contrasts, with facebrick surfaces adding earthy shades and textures to green leaves and bushes.

SIZE AND SCALE

Having established the importance of proportion in the garden plan as a whole, it follows that any masonry structure you decide to build should be designed to a suitable scale. If it is not,

the scheme will lack balance and unity. Generally, the size of any design should complement the house and the garden. However there are not many unbreakable rules in garden design, and you will need to assess how the brick structure you plan to build will fit into the space available.

It seems obvious that minimal structures fit small spaces and that you need a large spread to build something on a grand scale. While this is a safe and obvious route for most people to follow, it is also possible

A carefully planned brick patio incoporates a pergola, built-in seating, and a cooking area.

Red brick has been used to create harmony on a patio with several permanent structures.

to create cosy corners alongside a mansion, and you may well be able to build an extensive outdoor entertainment area beside a little cottage without it looking odd. In the latter instance, you will need to consider the scale of pergola pillars, built-in seating, and any other brick features very carefully. Built-in seating around the entire perimeter of a large patio which adjoins a small dwelling will make the area look like a public arena, while an enormous barbecue with a towering chimney will simply look out of place. Designing small features which mirror the size and scale of the house can also be a problem if the hard (or paved) surface of the patio is relatively large. The answer may be to aim for a focal point in one section of the patio. In this way, you may be able successfully to create a series of features in this area.

Apart from the relative sizes of the buildings and other structures on your property, it is also important to consider what various features will look like from several vantage points, both inside and outside the house. Avoid any design which may reduce the amount of sunlight reaching the interior of your house, or a structure which obscures an attractive view or vista across the garden.

If you want to build something in order to block an ugly outlook, your approach will, naturally, be quite different. Perhaps you are planning to erect a screen wall with a decorative fountain in brick. This should be positioned not only to hide the offending outlook but to be an attractive feature as well.

Some brick structures, including feature walls, pergolas, and walkways, may be used to divide the garden at certain points. A clever design, constructed near the boundary, may even create the impression that the garden continues a lot further than it actually does. Adapting the Japanese concept of optical illusion will enable you to build a feature on a larger scale that might otherwise have seemed inappropriate, as the garden will seem to continue beyond the structure.

BUILDING AN OUTDOOR KITCHEN

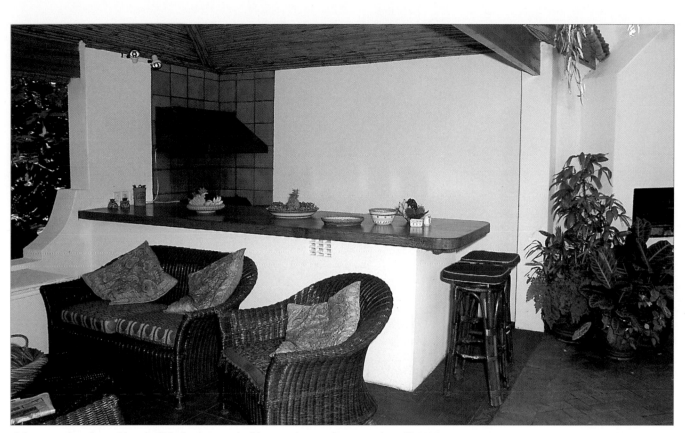

A bar counter alongside a built-in barbecue doubles as storage for several appliances.

While a patio designed for entertaining may simply consist of a paved surface with seating and perhaps a pergola for shade, an outdoor kitchen requires a lot more detail, including the need for cooking and storage facilities.

The basic elements of designing a barbecue structure are discussed on page 20. By extending the plan to include additional features, you will certainly increase its usefulness.

There are numerous features you can include in an outdoor kitchen. Instead of a barbecue unit where food is always cooked over the coals, consider a simple spit or battery-operated rotisserie. These are easily available and will increase the range of dishes you can cook. Pizza ovens and smaller baking ovens are other options, although you will need to be sure you have adequate bricklaying skills to tackle these projects. Unless properly constructed, with the inclusion of fire bricks, a chimney, and, in the case of a baking oven, a solid door, they will not work properly. You may also consider incorporating a hotplate to keep meals hot.

One of the most important design details of any barbecue unit is the fire bed, where cooking takes place. It is essential that this surface can withstand the intense heat of the fire, or you could find the whole structure cracking and even collapsing. The first step is to ensure that the surface where the fire will be made is flat and stable. While there is nothing to stop you from using the upper surface of a solid structure built to the required height, this will be wasted brickwork, unless, perhaps, the barbecue is built into an adjacent wall.

Instead, most designs feature a fire bed over an open area between the side walls of the structure. This is an ideal space for storing firewood, especially if the unit has an enclosed back wall as well. You can use a reinforced precast or galvanized steel lintel to span the space, or a precast concrete slab; otherwise you could cast concrete using a form (shuttering), which ideally should be reinforced as well.

Once this is in place, the secret is to top the concrete with a material which will not crack once a fire has been lit. Clay bricks or pavers, which are fired to very high

temperatures during the manufacturing process, are best. Alternatively, you can use special fire bricks, although these are relatively costly and not really necessary if good quality clay bricks are available. You could also top the slab with a buffer layer of soft sand, and then fit a metal ash tray, similar to those used for some indoor fireplaces. The advantage of these is that they can be removed whenever you want to clean up the coals, so you avoid having to sweep the coals off a fixed brick surface.

Other fittings also simplify the task of cooking outdoors. For instance, some people favor the inclusion of gas or electrical supplies and even a sink unit alongside the working surface. If these connections are to be provided, they should be supplied by licensed professionals. It is a relatively easy task, however, to install the necessary conduits and pipework.

While many barbecue structures are located in the open, elaborate designs are usually more successful in a sheltered spot on the patio. The site you choose will depend on your needs and on the options available for your spread.

A bricked-in precast pond is tiled for effect.

This simple brick structure incorporates seating, a small table, planter, and screen wall.

TYPE

The range of brick structures suitable for a garden, courtyard, or patio is limited only by your imagination, your budget, and the practical consideration of your building skills. Although bricklaying skills are easy to acquire, an amateur bricklayer who has never tackled a project before is advised to stick to something simple. If you take it one step at a time, you may eventually master even the most elaborate design. At the other end of the scale, an engineer who wants to do some home improvement can probably set his sights a little higher, with his greater knowledge of the principles and techniques involved.

The range of ideas that follow are aimed to appeal to a wide spectrum of home handymen. It is up to you to set the limits.

Planters

A brick planter is one of the simplest projects to tackle and as a feature it can be very effective, almost transforming a stark patio.

In a flat, uninteresting garden, a series of planters will enable you to create raised, or even tiered, levels or to divide a boring space, in this way creating interest and form. If you plant large foliage plants, you will eventually create an attractive screen, while flowers will add a splash of color.

In cases where you are faced with the prospect of a long, plain wall, either on the boundary or within the garden itself, the addition of planters in the design will immediately create visual interest. They may also be included in the layout of an outdoor stairway, or built on either side of a couple of steps, possibly at the entrance to the house or the approach to a garden terrace.

In an elaborate patio design, planters may also feature alongside built-in seating, tables, or a barbecue structure. Planted with striking or colorful species, a planter can become the main decorative feature of an area.

Far easier to maintain than pots and other free-standing containers, built-in planters are particularly useful in areas with poor soil conditions. They are also useful where drainage is a problem, because the base may be filled with broken bricks and stones, and weepholes or drainage pipes incorporated to lead water away from the roots of the plants.

Since quality soil of any type may be used to fill a planter, you can often introduce species which would not usually thrive in the environment of your garden. You must be sure, though, that the size of the container is suitable for the plants you choose.

Large shrubs or trees with spreading roots should be avoided.

Water features

Bricks and blocks are ideal materials for the construction of formal ponds and fountains. They may be used to build up the sides of water features, raising them above ground level, so that floating and marginal plants, as well as fish and other creatures, are easier to locate and watch. Alternatively, a low pond (possibly only one or two bricks high) may form a basin below a wall which has been fitted with a gargoyle or some other fountain head. You may even consider the possibility of a wishing well, particularly if you live in a quaint cottage-style home.

An imaginative design may include planters or even adjacent seating which will provide a place to view the fish. Sometimes the edge of the pool itself may double as an informal seating area. This is particularly suited to an ornamental Nishikigoi or koi pond where the colors and shapes of the fish are the focal point.

Masonry may also be used to construct informal ponds, but natural stone or reconstituted stone blocks are generally more suitable materials than bricks, as they have a much less formal appearance.

A major factor when building water features in brick is the question of waterproofing. If the inner surface is not properly sealed, the pond or pool will leak. The most effective procedure is to render the inner surface with mortar, to which a waterproofing compound has been added, and then to paint on bitumen or some other suitable nontoxic sealant.

The outside of a brick pond may also be rendered, depending upon the effect you wish to create.

Seating and built-in furniture

Any furniture intended to be left outside permanently must be made from a material which will last and not deteriorate in wet or other extreme conditions. Masonry is therefore an obvious choice. It can be combined with other materials, including lumber, which makes a sensible but attractive surface for both seats and tables. Alternatively, brickwork can be filled in and the tops of some furniture designs can be tiled, topped with concrete, or reconstituted stone slabs, or even finished with brick paving.

The location of permanent outdoor furniture will depend on your personal requirements. For example, you may want somewhere to relax away from the house, or perhaps a place where family and friends can use as an outdoor retreat for a drink or meal, without having to lug chairs, stools, and tables with them.

Some types of movable furniture may be left outside in all weathers, but built-in benches and tables are a very useful addition to a patio. The simplest designs comprise supporting walls which provide a base for table tops and timber seating. Set against a wall, a bench will automatically have a back and all you will need is a few pillows to provide a comfortable place to relax. Simply remove the pillows when the furniture is not in use.

There is no reason why furniture constructed in brick should not be located in the garden itself. A bench tucked away in a corner which faces colorful flower beds, a rose garden, or a water feature, will encourage you to spend time enjoying these visual

An elaborate patio design with built-in furniture and a practical barbecue shelf is perfect for home-cooked meals and entertaining.

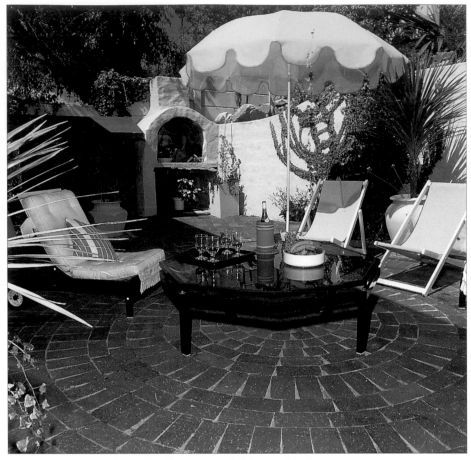

A plastered brick barbecue is a feature on a brick-paved patio.

located, but also on your construction skills. A simple arrangement will involve little more than building a series of walls, and once you have mastered basic bricklaying, you should have no difficulty with it. Incorporating a chimney takes a little more experience and ability, and the addition of an oven (either for pizzas or for baking bread) demands considerable expertise. Make sure you are familiar with all the techniques required before you tackle a project which could become hard work.

Siting a barbecue correctly is important as it will affect the use you get out of it. It should be out of the wind, accessible to the house (especially the kitchen), and positioned near a seating area where family and friends are likely to gather. Ensure it is well clear of large trees, as the overhanging branches may be a fire hazard.

Smoke is inevitably a problem, particularly on a confined or partially enclosed patio, but this can be minimized by an efficient chimney which will draw smoke away from the area.

pleasures. If the bench is topped with a material such as granite or mosaic, it will become a feature in its own right.

The size and dimensions of outdoor furniture will depend on the function you expect it to fulfill. A long bench, for instance, will require intermediate supporting pillars to prevent the seat from sagging.

If a table is located alongside seating, it is important to ensure that the height of the seat is compatible with the height of the table top. Seating should be close enough to the ground to enable feet to rest comfortably on the surface below, while the table should be positioned in such a way that it can be used for meals and with sufficient space to get in behind it.

Benches may be built in on either side of a table, or you can use portable seating on one side. The latter option can be more versatile if you entertain regularly, since you can vary the seating arrangement and the table will also be accessible for buffet meals.

Seating arrangements do not have to be elaborate; even a single wood-topped seat alongside a pond or planter can be both functional and esthetically pleasing.

Barbecue structures

Anybody who enjoys an alfresco meal is sure to delight in the opportunity to cook outdoors. People all over the world enjoy meals prepared over an open fire, using a variety of both portable and permanent units. If the idea appeals to you, a built-in barbecue will add an enjoyable element to outdoor entertaining.

Ideally, the structure will include a reasonable working surface (even if you prepare the food in the kitchen, you will want somewhere to put the dishes), seating, and storage space for firewood, cooking equipment, and maybe gas cylinders or Sterno™ cans.

The design you choose will depend not only on your requirements and the environment in which it is to be

Storage units and garden utilities

Surprisingly few people consider the advantage of building simple storage units on patios or in the garden. Those that are most common occur in utility areas and are used to house or screen garbage cans, store swimming pool equipment, or shelter firewood. They are generally plain, unexciting, and sometimes rather unattractive and do little to improve the appeal of the outdoor area.

Imaginatively planned, outdoor storage for pillows, barbecue equipment, such as gas cylinders, pool items, and even smaller gardening implements (trowel, shears, gloves, and so on) may be incorporated in the patio plan. All that is needed is a watertight box with a securely fitting lid, shelving which is sheltered from the elements, or a right-angled wall which could incorporate a planter to screen a garbage can. If you are building a barbecue, consider fronting

TRADITIONAL GARDEN STRUCTURES

Since stone is a natural material and brick has been used for thousands of years, it is not surprising that many traditional garden structures and buildings are built with various types of masonry.

Garden houses of earlier ages were built in brick or stone in Europe, and in wood in 18th century North America. Garden structures were a feature of the homes of the wealthy, their styles varying from country to country and changing through the ages. The ancient Romans were known to have used marble for some of their garden houses, and some beautiful banqueting houses, used purely for entertaining, were built from local stone in England during the Tudor period. Often these were sited at some distance from the house and used either for festive occasions or as a secret retreat from the world.

Follies, which enjoyed their heyday in 18th century Britain, were also built from masonry, most frequently stone. They took various forms, from temples and pyramids to structures deliberately made to look like ruined buildings. They had no real use except to catch the eye and perhaps to act as a temporary shelter for visitors touring the property. These too, were found only in the gardens of the wealthy, but smaller versions were designed by a number of Victorian landscape gardeners.

One of the most charming garden buildings of the 19th century was built by the renowned English garden designer, Gertrude Jekyll. Known as The Thunder House (and designed by the equally renowned architect, Sir Edwin Lutyens), it is a plain gazebo-like structure built from local stone (as was the house), and was often used in Miss Jekyll's day to watch the progress of summer thunder storms!

The gazebo is perhaps the most time-honored garden structure. It is usually built of stone or brick and was traditionally sited at one corner of a property or on a terrace. It was often raised so that it could capture the view beyond. Designed in a square, hexagonal or octagonal shape, the gazebo generally features a steeply pitched roof which was traditionally covered with slate, shake, or sometimes thatch.

There are much-photographed traditional gazebos all over the world, many of which have survived for hundreds or even thousands of years. Apart from Gertrude Jekyll's Thunder House, another famous design was by an American, Lawrence Johnston, who built a square, brick gazebo

with a shingled roof in the garden of his Hidcote Manor home in England.

Summerhouses too, were frequently built from stone or brick. More reclusive and less open than a gazebo, a summerhouse was the place to sit on warm summer days. Although today's summerhouse is often used for temporary accommodation, the traditional type was generally too open and offered only partial shelter. By the mid-19th century, wood was a more common material than masonry for this kind of structure.

On a larger scale, the pavilion (originally just a tent in the ancient Orient) became a far more substantial structure in 18th century France. In fact, it could be called the royalty's version of the garden shed! Some pavilions were large enough to be used as guest houses, while others were used to accommodate a favored mistress. Although these grand pavilions were built of masonry, later designs (including the park bandstand) were commonly made of wood.

On a more practical level, a range of utility buildings, designed for housing animals, storing tools, and keeping fruits and other foods, became popular in Europe during

the 19th century. One of the most interesting was the French *ferme orné*, meaning "ornamental farm." In England. these solid structures were used to disguise what might have been ugly, utilitarian buildings.

Probably the oldest garden building built of brick or masonry was the dovecote, designed for keeping pigeons and doves. The ancient Romans are believed to have invented this structure, designing rounded stone towers with nest holes and little shelves built into the walls from the ground all the way to the top.

In both France and early England, elaborate dovecotes were constructed from stone, while in colonial America, attractive brick dovecotes were a feature in some of the grander gardens. In South Africa, thickly plastered and whitewashed ones are found in the grounds of some of the early Cape Dutch manor houses.

Nowadays these bird houses are more commonly set on a single post and are frequently made of wood.

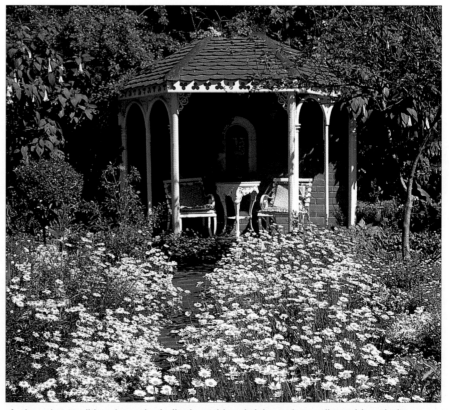

A charming traditional gazebo built alongside a brick garden wall provides shelter.

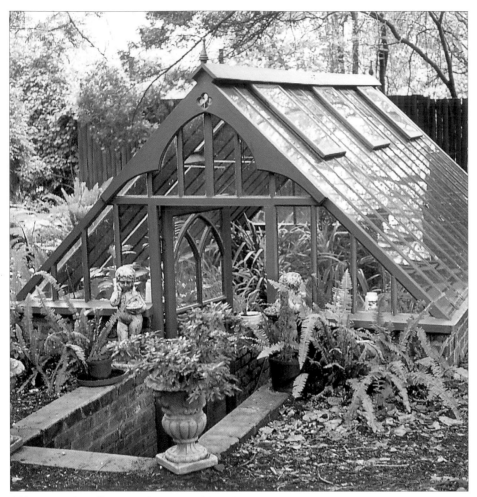

This unusual sunken greenhouse combines brick walls and a wood-and-glass roof.

a section of the unit with doors. This can be used for items which could blow away or deteriorate if they get wet. Firewood, on the other hand, may be stacked below the surface which forms the fire bed, even if it is partially open to the elements.

The materials chosen to front an outdoor cupboard or to cover a brick container will have a major effect on the design. Lumber is the first choice, but it should be sealed or painted to improve its appearance as well as to increase its lifespan.

Garbage can screens and similar structures are functional and they do hide unsightly items from view, but it is important to ensure that they look as though they fit in with the design of the outdoor area in which they are located. If a brick wall adjacent to a storage unit has been rendered with mortar and then painted, it is advisable to use the same finish on the garbage

can shelter. If it is built next to a wood fence, match the door of the storage unit to the lumber used for the fence.

Although wood and wire are the most common materials for composters, brick is a suitable option. Since circulating air is essential for the waste vegetable and plant material to break down, it is best to use pierced screen blocks or to build the walls using bricks laid in a honeycomb pattern, leaving gaps between the ends of each brick. Ideally, a composter should have two or even three compartments so that as one heap decomposes, you can start composting the next one off.

Pergolas and gazebos

Pergolas and other overhead shelters (sometimes referred to as arbors), are common on patios, whether they are located alongside the house, in the garden, or beside an activity area

such as a tennis court or pool. Pergolas consist of upright pillars, poles, or posts with lighter overhead beams and crosspieces. They are sometimes built against the wall of the house (which provides a support at one end or along one side.) Some are roofed (see pages 26–27), while others are left open or used as a support for climbing plants.

A variety of materials can be used for the uprights of a pergola, but masonry is undoubtedly one of the more popular options. The design should be in harmony with existing architectural influences and the proportions in keeping with the size of the spread, as well as existing garden features and other buildings on the property.

A well-designed carport may also feature brick pillars, but the roof is often more solid than that of a pergola.

Although most modern gazebos are probably built of wood or metal, brick is an option which may be considered for more solid side-walls, even if these only extend halfway up the structure. When combined with brick pillars, a design of this type can be an unusual and attractive feature in the contemporary garden.

Play structures

Although the majority of play structures are built out of lumber, there is nothing to stop you building a playhouse from bricks and mortar. In fact, this a perfect project to build as practicen for anyone who has the basic skills and who is planning to try their hand at some more challenging bricklaying, such as a garden building or a boundary wall which incorporates planters.

Bricks may be used to build a simple structure such as a sandpit for young children. It need be no larger than 5 feet x 5 feet and no more than three courses high. A sandpit could be positioned where it could later look attractive if filled with shrubs and flowers, so that it can be used until your children tire of it and then easily converted into a planter.

It is essential to ensure that the sub-base of any sandpit will allow water to drain away naturally. If it does not, it will turn into a swamp after heavy rain. It is also a good idea to cover a sandpit when not in use to prevent cats and dogs from fouling the sand.

Garden buildings

Few people today can afford the type of garden buildings which were created during the 16th–18th centuries in Europe and Britain as banqueting halls or secret hideaways. However, there are numerous, quite simple garden structures which may be built from bricks, blocks, and similar materials.

Toolsheds and outdoor workrooms built from brick will provide you with a permanent place to carry out home handyman projects which would make a mess elsewhere. Greenhouses and conservatories can also be built from brick, with glass panels or a glass or polycarbonate roof to let in sunlight.

Barns and animal shelters may also be built from bricks and mortar. In fact, masonry is the ideal material for this type of building, particularly if it is to house horses, cattle, or other animals. Not only will it provide a solid, stable shelter, but it can be cleaned easily by hosing it down with water.

Changing rooms can be useful beside a swimming pool on a large property. They can be planned to accommodate pool cleaning equipment, pumps, filters, chlorination units, and recreational items such as inflatable matresses, beach balls, and folding outdoor furniture.

There are various roofing possibilities for all of these buildings. The most suitable types include sheeting in its many guises, shake, and tiles. Thatch is another option, though it is extremely hard to find in the U.S. Shake and thatch are potential fire hazards, unless properly fireproofed.

STYLE

There is no doubt that small buildings and other structures will contribute to the general style and character of your garden. If your house has a definite style, try to emulate it, and devise a scheme which will complement it rather than compete with it. For instance, a period clapboard house will benefit from features such as a small, modern dovecote, an informal pond, arches, and perhaps even a wishing-well. A Victorian-style garden will demand a traditional gazebo for authenticity, while one in the Japanese style will gain character from natural stone seating. The larger English-style garden can usually accommodate a range of structures, including a traditional pergola. If your house is a clean-lined one built in facebrick, it is usually best to match the materials as well as the style.

A thatched shelter built with bricks and mortar is an unusual outdoor entertaining option.

MATERIAL OPTIONS

There is a surprisingly wide choice of materials for garden structures which are to be built in masonry. Both clay and concrete bricks are manufactured in a range of colors and finishes, and concrete blocks are available either hollow, pierced, or in the form of reconstructed or reconstituted stone. Some types of bricks or blocks are intended to be left as they are, while others should be rendered with mortar and then painted.

In some parts of the U.S., clay and/or adobe blocks are available, and many of the structures suggested can also be built with natural stone.

Clay and concrete bricks

Available as facebricks for rendering or plastering, these materials are a popular choice for garden masonry structures. There is a wide range of colors and textures to choose from, which means you are sure to find something that will suit any garden environment. Brick sizes are relatively standard, varying slightly from country to country. They are relatively small and therefore easy to handle, making them the perfect choice for the amateur builder.

Your choice of brick will depend largely upon the style and character of the structure you are building. The most expensive option is clay facebrick (also called facing-brick) which is strong and long-lasting in all weather conditions – an important consideration in areas which experience severe frost, snow, or constant sea spray. You will find that specifications differ, and where conditions are harsh, it is wise to check durability factors with your supplier or manufacturer.

Concrete facebricks are also available in a range of textures and colors, although these are not as natural as the hues of clay brick.

If you plan to render the surface of your structure, it makes sense to use non-face bricks (or non-facings). These are much less expensive than facebricks, but are not intended to be left unprotected.

Concrete blocks

Standard blocks, manufactured in a reasonably wide range of sizes, are a cost-effective option. Not only are they less expensive than bricks (when compared per square foot), but these hollow units are also quicker to lay because they are larger.

As ordinary concrete blocks are not particularly attractive, in most instances you will need to render (plaster) the finished surface. Another possibility is to camouflage the structure with a brick veneer, although this will involve additional work and will also increase costs because of the extra materials required.

Screen blocks

A range of attractive screen blocks with pierced patterns may be used within the garden. Commonly used for

Attractive facebricks have been used to build a quaint arched entrance and matching boundary wall.

both boundary and screen walls, these units allow both light and air to pass through the structure. Since they are laid in a stack bond, which is not particularly strong (see page 32), they are only suitable for certain applications, where intermediate piers help support them.

Pierced blocks could be used to construct a simple composter, provided the pattern of holes is not too open.

Reconstituted (reconstructed) stone blocks

Manufactured from concrete in imitation of stone, reconstituted stone blocks and smaller brick-like units are a good idea for all types of garden structures and buildings, as long as they match the style of your garden and existing structures. Colors and textures are chosen to blend with natural stonework, and sizes to correspond to the typical dimensions of cut (ashlar) stone.

An advantage of building with reconstituted stone rather than the genuine material is that these blocks are considerably easier to lay because of their regular shapes and sizes. Large jumper blocks, which are the height of two courses, are sometimes available in a variety of different sizes, for an authentic look.

Clay and adobe blocks

Although clay blocks are fired in the same way as clay bricks, adobe blocks are manufactured in quite a different way, and are only available in the Southwest (Texas, Arizona, and New Mexico.) Traditional adobe structures eventually deteriorate, but nowadays these blocks are stabilized with asphalt, cement, or straw to prevent them from crumbling and decomposing. Aobe blocks are larger than clay bricks (and even some clay blocks), and therefore relatively cumbersome to work with because they are so heavy.

Stone

The craft of stonemasonry is an ancient one which has been passed down through the ages in just about

A combination of stone and brick works well.

every country in the world. Whether you use cut or dressed stone, or lay irregular rocks in a random pattern, the effects obtained will add charm to any garden. Stone is suitable for many garden features, although it is considerably more difficult to lay than brick and block.

Various types of stone are found in different areas. Your choice will depend on availability.

ROOFING POSSIBILITIES

Brick pergolas, gazebos, walkways, and various garden buildings built with masonry units, may incorporate simple roofs which offer some shelter from the sun, rain, and wind. A shed or summerhouse will, of necessity, have a roof which provides a greater degree of protection than the average pergola.

It is not surprising that the type of roof chosen will depend largely on the degree of shelter you require from the elements. Awning fabric (shadecloth), for instance, will be quite adequate for a pergola which will provide shade, while a toolshed will demand something much more substantial. A gazebo traditionally incorporates a tiled or asbestos shake roof, while a summerhouse might be roofed in wooden shingles for an old-fashioned look.

As with all other materials, the type of roofing you choose must complement the materials used elsewhere. This does not mean you necessarily have

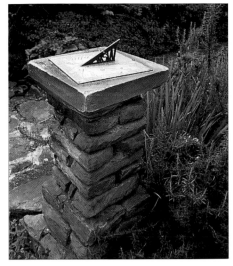

Sundial on a concrete slab set on stone.

to match the roof to your house, but any new material you introduce should blend well with it.

The supporting structure of the roof will depend on what it will cover and the load it will bear. However, specific structural elements are not considered in any detail here as more substantial buildings will require greater expertise than is necessary for the projects discussed in this book.

Plants

If you do not want to cover a pergola or similar overhead structure with roofing, plants should always be considered. You will find that a wide variety of climbers and creepers are suitable for this purpose. Not only will they make the structure look attractive, but flowering species will also add color, and many types will have a delightful fragrance as well. A pergola is an effective structure for supporting plants. If properly trained, they will soon form a charming, natural ceiling.

The type or types of plant you choose will depend on what is suitable to your local climate. Climbers and creepers include honeysuckle, jasmine, and rambling roses Clematis, wisteria, Virginia creeper, and grapevines will all lose their leaves in winter, but this allows the sun to filter into an area which might otherwise become cold, damp, and unusable in the cool season. Of course, any climbing plants you choose will take time to grow.

Awning material

Awning material is available in various guises and is a good choice for pergolas located on patios which require some shade. Although some types are water-resistant, most are not waterproof and will therefore not give any protection from the rain.

Most retractable awnings are made from canvas, which is available in many different colors, both plain and patterned (usually striped.)

Shadecloth, made from a hardy acrylic material and sold throughout the U.S., is available in a variety of fashion colors, as well as in green and black, the hues more commonly used for horticultural purposes. Various densities offer anything from 30% to 85% protection from the sun's rays. This material should be cut with a soldering iron to prevent it from fraying and should never be placed over lumber that has been treated with creosote, as this will cause it to deteriorate.

Roofing felt

Bituminous roofing felt is a reasonably inexpensive option particularly suitable for sheds, carports, and utility buildings. It is usually sold in rolls and nailed to plywood, hardboard, particle board, masonite, or whatever other boarding has been used over the roof trusses or battens.

Although this material has a reasonably long lifespan, it may need to be resealed with a bituminous waterproofing compound from time to time. Odd holes, including those created by nails, may be sealed with bitumen paste or mastic.

Roof sheeting

A wide range of sheeting is suitable for the roofs of all kinds of garden buildings. Some types are available as flat sheets, but most are corrugated. All types are suitable for brick buildings with roofs that have a minimum pitch of 5-10°, although cost will probably determine what you choose for a simple shed or animal shelter. If sheeting is used for a pitched roof, you will have to fix capping along the ridge.

A combination of reeds and plants form the roof of this simple, rendered pergola.

If it is used for a structure which abuts a building, you will need to seal the join with flashing to prevent rain and moisture from seeping through the gap. Remember, too, that whatever kind of roof sheeting you are using, the sheets must overlap at the joins. Some will need to be predrilled prior to installation, although self-drilling roofing screws are usually sufficient.

One of the cheapest kinds of roof sheeting is fiberglass, which is suitable not only for a range of small garden buildings but also for open-sided structures like pergolas and carports. Lightweight and easy to handle, it is available in several different profiles and a range of translucent colors.

Polycarbonate, a smooth, synthetic material which looks like glass or perspex, is better suited to pergolas and conservatory-type extensions. It comes in flat or corrugated sheets, and is available in the same sheet sizes as fiberglass and metal.

Another lightweight, corrugated variety of sheeting is Onduline™ which is manufactured in France from organic fibers which have been saturated in bitumen. It is widely distributed and available in brown, black, bottle green, red, and translucent. It is a good choice for outbuildings and overhead structures which require a solid roof.

Both corrugated iron and aluminum sheeting (which is also used for some awnings) may be used, but the latter is a relatively expensive option, particularly for an outbuilding. Special tools are required to cut it, and because it is relatively "soft" it is easily damaged. For this reason it is generally installed by professionals. On the other hand, iron, which is available galvanized or color-coated, is reasonably priced and particularly popular for carports.

Although heavy, fibercement is another option which is usually relatively inexpensive. It is manufactured in a selection of profiles and requires sturdy roof trusses and carport beams, depending, of course, on where it is to be used.

Tiles, shingles, and shakes

Many traditional garden buildings constructed with bricks and mortar or stone had roofs which were finished in tile, slates, or shingles. Today, garden buildings of all kinds are roofed with these materials, provided that they have a minimum pitch of 15–26°. Generally the rougher the finish, the greater the pitch required.

Flat slate and clay tiles, as well as shingles and shakes (made from wood, asphalt, aluminum, or glass fiber), or thicker wooden shingles are good choices for a gazebo roof.

Roofing tiles, made from various materials including clay, fibercement and reconstituted stone, may be used, to cover outbuildings, summerhouses, sheds, and simple pitched pergolas.

Thatch

Suitable for pitched pergolas and some garden buildings, thatch requires a minimum pitch of about 45°. It is a popular choice for open-sided summerhouses in some hot climates, and comes in many traditional designs, but it can only be installed by skilled craftsmen. If you favor this material, you will need to ensure that the roof structure is made with wooden poles rather than sawn lumber.

If natural thatch is not available you could use acrylic thatch.

Reeds, bamboo, and lumber

Attached to the crossbeams of a pergola, these natural materials will produce attractive dappled shadows, and provide shade as well as some shelter from the wind and light rain. Bamboo and reeds may also be used for the ceiling of a garden building (possibly a summerhouse or a shelter for entertaining) or on a patio which has a more substantial roof.

Lumber is the most common of these three materials, since it is available everywhere and easier to render fireproof and insectproof. Laths may be arranged across the beams in a regular row, as closely or widely spaced as you wish. Obviously the smaller the gaps between the lengths of lumber, the more shade and shelter you will have. If the laths are too close, this can make an enclosed area look dark and gloomy. As an alternative to straight laths, a pergola may be topped with latticework, which you can make yourself or buy readymade.

Where reeds and bamboo are available, these materials make charming patio roofs. If they are not available from a store, there may be a supplier in your area who has access to the material in the field. If you cannot track anyone down, try advertising in the classified section of your local newspaper.

In some areas you can buy bamboo in woven rolls, ready for installation. If you can't find these, string the stalks together to form your own panels, or attach them directly to the pergola beams. You should use green material that has not yet dried out, since this prevents it from splitting and ensures that the lengths fit neatly side-by-side. You can either tie the lengths in place, or predrill them before nailing them to the lumber. Set the reeds with thick and thin ends alternating, to ensure an even finish.

LIGHTING

Although not every garden is illuminated at night, some form of exterior lighting is essential, not only for safety, but for security as well. It is dangerous if you cannot see where you are going, and if you cannot detect intruders.

It makes sense to install lighting in most garden buildings, especially if you want to make use of them in the evenings. If they are situated some distance from the house, you may require additional wiring. You can probably lay low-voltage cables and fix fittings yourself, but the mains connection should be made by a registered electrician.

Patios should also be illuminated, and those which are attached to the house often make use of existing fittings. You will need good general lighting, rather than spotlights or uplighters. Where new fittings are installed, these must be suitable for outdoor use – most lighting stores have a good selection of sealed units from which to choose.

Features in the garden are usually illuminated at night for decorative purposes only. Uplighters are used for highlighting foliage and steps, and generally use low-voltage systems.

An open brick building has a thatched roof installed by a skilled craftsman.

A thorough knowledge and understanding of basic building principles is essential for anyone tackling an outdoor project in brick. Not only is it essential to know the right techniques for laying bricks and ensuring they are properly bonded, but it is also important for structures to be square, level, and plumb.

An experienced bricklayer knows the value of using the correct tools and appreciates the importance of working with the right concrete and mortar mixes. If your structure is to look professional, it is vital that you familiarize yourself with these elements. It is also useful to have some basic knowledge of quantifying materials, so that you can cost the project reasonably accurately and avoid the unnecessary wastage which is so often incurred when ordering is based on guesswork.

THE ESSENTIAL TOOLKIT

Although certain very specific tools are required for bricklaying, the essential toolkit is not extensive. All items are available at building supply stores, hardware stores, and major home improvement outlets.

In addition to those listed below, you will need a spade to excavate the earth, possibly a shovel to mix concrete and mortar (although you can also use a spade), a pick if the ground is hard or stony, and a wheelbarrow to transport bricks, mixed materials, and excess soil to and from the excavation.

If you are planning to incorporate wooden seat tops or wooden lids and closet doors into your brick structure, you will also need a basic carpentry kit, with saws, a drill, screwdrivers, and a hammer. A combination square (sometimes referred to as a carpenter's square) is also useful.

Compactors

A punner, or ramming tool, is handy for compacting the earth or fill beneath footings. It can be made by filling an empty 5-quart paint can with concrete, and inserting a pole or length of lumber as a handle. The flat end of a fairly heavy round pole may be used instead, but if you need to compact a large area, it is advisable to hire a compacting machine.

Straightedge

Invaluable for extending the usefulness of a spirit level over large areas, a straightedge may be made of metal or wood. If wood is chosen, make certain it is not warped or bowed. A straightedge may also be used for compacting and smoothing concrete, for leveling mortar on a rendered surface, and as a gauge rod.

Tape measure

A good quality, retractable steel tape is the builder's best friend, as it is used from the setting-out stage, until completion of the project.

Gauge rod

An invaluable aid for keeping brick and block courses regular, a gauge rod is simply a flat, straight-edged length of lumber or metal which is marked off according to the height of each course, at intervals equal to one brick or block plus a mortar joint. Some professionals mark their spirit level in the appropriate gauges, so they do not have to use two tools during bricklaying. The dimensions chosen will depend on the size of the masonry unit you are using as well as the thickness of the mortar joints. A foolproof method is to lay the first two courses and then to use this to guide you when marking it off.

Framing square

This is a tool no bricklayer should be without. A framing or builder's square is made of steel and is marked off like

A selection of items required for the basic toolkit of anyone planning to tackle bricklaying.

A builder's square is an essential tool to ensure that all corners are at 90˚.

a ruler. The framing or builder'ssquare (also known as a carpenter's square), enables you to check that all corners are at 90˚.

When setting out a structure, you may find that a framing square is not big enough; if so, you can make a larger one out of wood, using the 3:4:5 method (see below and page 37). Make sure that the angle you create is correct or your structure will not be square.

Spirit level

The spirit level is another indispensable tool and is used at every stage of the building process to ensure that foundations and both horizontal and vertical brick surfaces are level and plumb. This metal tool incorporates both a horizontal and a vertical vial. If the bubble is in the center, the surface is level. When laying out a drainage slope, you can put a block of wood under one end of the level to achieve the required slope (see below). A line level, which is basically a vial without a straight-edged metal casing, may be strung onto a builder's line (also known as a chalk line) and used as an additional aid but it cannot be used to check for plumb.

Line and pins or corner block

A builder's line (or string) is used with wooden or metal pegs to set out the foundations for brick structures. Not only is string very inexpensive, it is also easier to see than a builder's line.When laying bricks, builder's line is strung along the upper level of the course to be laid. It may be used in conjunction with metal pins or with corner blocks (see page 31). Other-wise, you can simply wind the line around a brick to secure it.

Trowels, mortarboards, and floats

A standard bricklaying trowel is essential for laying the bricks, while a rectangular plasterer's trowel is used when rendering walls. Although not essential, corner trowels are a useful addition to the toolkit. Shaped to fit either outside or inside corners, they simplify the task of neatening the vertical edges of a rendered structure. A mortarboard or screedboard (or hawk) is useful, but certainly not high on the list of priorities for the essential toolkit. Many professionals use this tool to hold small quantities of mortar while they lay the bricks or render the surface. When working at ground level, you can simply dip into the wheel-barrow. Alternatively, use a flat piece of metal or board.

If the surface is to be rendered, you will need to purchase a wooden float to smooth the mortar once it has been laid on. A steel float is not generally used for external walls.

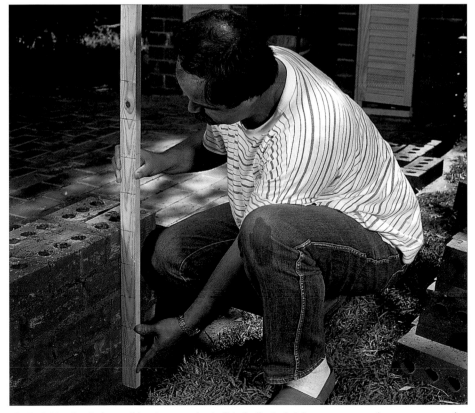

A straight-edged piece of lumber, marked off to indicate brick courses, used as a gauge rod.

Pointing and jointing tools

Various pointing and jointing tools are used to place mortar in the joints and to rake it out, respectively. A pointing trowel (which looks like a small-scale bricklayer's trowel) is normally used to fill in small holes in the mortar. If you "butter" the ends of the bricks properly as you work, you should be able to manage without one.

While a narrow trowel or special jointer may be used to finish both vertical and horizontal joints, a piece of metal, cut to form a square tip, is quite adequate. Traditionally joints were finished in various ways. They could be either concave, flush, recessed to a square finish, or even jointed so that the mortar protruded slightly. There is an art to these

A float is used to screed a concrete slab.

techniques, and the home handyman need do no more than rake out the excess mortar to neaten the joint.

Brick-cutting tools

There are several options for cutting bricks. Probably the simplest is to use a brick hammer, which has a chisel end for this purpose, although it does not always cut neatly, especially if you are not adept at handling it. A bolster or broad chisel may be used instead. Place the brick on the ground (preferably on a bed of sand) and score the surface to mark the required cutting line. Place the chisel blade on the line and knock firmly with a hefty club hammer. For very tough bricks, an electrically-powered angle grinder may be necessary.

Block-splitters and power-saws may be used for cutting larger concrete blocks; they may be hired if you do not want to buy one.

Rubber mallet

This rubber-headed hammer is also useful for tapping stubborn bricks into place. It will not damage the bricks.

Saws

Although not strictly part of the bricklayer's toolkit, a good-quality saw is essential if you are cutting lumber to make corner blocks, straightedges, and so on.

BUILDING PRINCIPLES

Any well-built brick structure must be square, level, and plumb. The exceptions, of course, are curved walls and circular structures, in which case there will obviously be no need to aim for right-angled corners.

Square

Any rectangular (or square) structure must have right-angled corners. If it does not, you will end up with crooked walls and a structure which is askew. For this reason, it is essential not only to set out the structure correctly (see below and page 37) but also to use a builder's square to check the corners regularly as the brickwork progresses. Never rely on your own judgement. Your workmanship may look absolutely square to you, but even the slightest inaccuracies can make a difference.

Level and plumb

Horizontal surfaces must be level, and vertical surfaces plumb. To ensure that they are, it is essential to check them at every stage. Make sure that the excavation is level, the foundation slab is absolutely flat, and the brickwork is even. It is vital not to rely on guesswork, otherwise you will have problems and may find yourself having to demolish what you have built.

The most common, and certainly the most versatile, tool used for this purpose is a spirit level. It will enable you to check both horizontal and vertical surfaces, at all stages and

A brick hammer is used to halve a brick.

An angle grinder is useful for cutting bricks.

A bolster and club hammer used together.

in all positions. For instance, as brickwork progresses, you can use a spirit level to check the upper surface of the bricks. By setting it on a straight-edged length of lumber, you can check that two corners are at the same height. You can also check the vertical sides of the bricks, to ensure that the wall of brickwork is rising square and true, and you can use it on the diagonal to make sure the

A spirit level is an essential tool to ensure that brickwork is level and plumb.

There are various ways of bonding brickwork. Several patterns which have been used for centuries. The simplest, which is also the most common, is known as stretcher (or running) bond.

Stretcher bond brickwork is achieved by laying bricks so that they overlap those in the course below by a half. Not only is the result attractive, but it is also very strong. It is also the only structurally sound bond which can be used to build a half-brick wall (comprising a single skin of brickwork), and the most economical when a cavity wall (with two rows of parallel brickwork) is constructed. Furthermore, it is the obvious choice when building a wall which is to be rendered, since there is little point in creating a fancy pattern which will not be visible. When a one-brick wall is built in facebrick, any of the other options may be used, as you will find that the patterns created are quite different to those made by using stretcher bond.

English bond, the strongest of all bonds, is created by laying alternate courses of headers and stretchers. A course of headers is laid across a double skin of brickwork, each brick placed at right angles to the main run of bricks, and exposing the end, or header, on the outer wall.

English garden wall bond is a variation of ordinary English bond and consists of a header course followed by three to five stretcher courses.

vertical surface is even.

A builder's line can also be used to keep brick courses level. Hooked onto the corner of the brickwork with a corner block, or attached by sticking special pins into the mortar, it creates a constant guide at whichever level you set it at. On a large expanse of wall, it may be used in conjunction with a line level.

Although corner blocks are sometimes available from stores, they are easily made from wood offcuts. You will need two 2X4s. Cut a section out of each 2X4 to form a chunky L-shape, and then saw half-way through the foot of the L to create a slot to hold the line in place. Wind the line around the base of the foot and draw it through the slot. The block is then hooked onto the corner of the brickwork at the correct height, and the line stretched to the opposite corner where it is attached to a second corner block.

Although a plumb bob may be used to check vertical surfaces at corners, it is really only useful on a large expanse of wall, for instance a highrise building.

Bonding

All bricks must be properly bonded so that the walls of the structure are strong and form a solid mass. This ensures that the load is distributed laterally along the entire length of the wall. If the brickwork is not bonded, the vertical joints (or perpends) will be in a straight line and the load will not be distributed at all.

Corner blocks, easily made from 2X4s, help keep brick courses straight.

Flemish bond consists of alternating headers and pairs of stretchers in the same course. The headers in the second course are centered over the stretchers of the first, and *vice versa*.

Flemish garden wall bond consists of a header followed by two or three pairs of stretchers in the same course.

MATERIALS

The basic ingredients of all masonry work are the same. You will need bricks, blocks, or stone, as well as mortar made with cement, sand, and water (and sometimes lime or plasticizer to bind the units together). You will also need concrete foundations or footings, made with cement, sand, a coarse aggregate, and water. Metal reinforcements may be required in the foundations or between the brickwork. Lumber may be required for seating, storage compartments, and closets, as well as for formwork when pouring or casting concrete slabs.

Bricks and blocks

Stretcher bond, is a common option.

English bond, probably the strongest bond.

English garden wall bond.

Flemish bond has headers and stretchers.

A single or half-brick wall constructed using a stretcher bond pattern.

Bricks and blocks are made of clay, concrete, or calcium silicate and are available in a range of standard size. Your choice will depend largely on what kind of structure you are building and whether it is to be rendered (plastered), and painted or left with the face of the brick showing.

Although reconstituted (reconstructed) stone blocks are solid, many other concrete blocks are hollow. Bricks, on the other hand, may have an indent (or frog) in one face, or they may contain two or three holes. Paving bricks are generally solid and flat. Both frogs and holes will aid bonding, and these characteristics are the result of different methods of manufacture. Indented bricks are molded, while the holes are caused by the more modern process of extrusion.

In addition to standard bricks and blocks, bricks shaped in various ways are available for finishing walls and other brickwork. Pavers (paving bricks) may be used to top a table or the worksurface of a barbecue or outdoor bar, while bullnosed bricks (which are rounded along one side or at one end) may be used to finish ends neatly. They are also useful for laying around ponds and other decorative features. Various coping (or capping) bricks are also available.

The quality of bricks varies considerably. For instance, those manufactured for general building work that is to be rendered may deteriorate if they are not coated with mortar. You will also find that there is some variation in the size and finish of different facebricks. Ask your supplier for information regarding those available in your area.

Apart from the bricks chosen to build your structure, you may decide to use firebricks on the cooking surface of a barbecue and tough engineering or exposure-grade bricks where walls are likely to be exposed to constant damp. If necessary, seek professional advice.

Cement

Ordinary cement, suitable for most concrete and mortar work, is sold in powder form, in sealed 100-pound (and sometimes 50-pound or 80-pound) paper-and-plastic sacks, and should be stored in a waterproof environment, preferably stacked above the ground and covered with plastic sheeting. If cement gets wet, it will become lumpy and unusable. Unless you are involved in a major building project, do not buy more cement than you can use within a maximum of three months.

Sand

Sold in volume or in open bags (usually containing about 50 or 100 pounds), sand must be of good quality and suitable for building. The best sands are evenly graded, containing particles of various sizes. Sand that does not contain sufficient fine material ("fines") will tend to produce a weak, porous surface layer if it is used for concrete. If sand is too fine, mortar will tend to rise to the surface of the concrete. If the particles are mostly the same size, the concrete will be difficult to work with.

Where sand is graded as "soft" and

Bricks come in a variety of shapes and sizes for both paving and construction work.

"sharp," you should use the soft sand for bricklaying and the coarser, sharp sand for making concrete. Where plaster sand is available, this contains lime and is suitable for making mortar for both bricklaying and rendering. Otherwise it is usually best to add your own lime or plasticizer (see page 34.)

Although the source of sand is not necessarily a foolproof guide, you will

Concrete blocks are laid with mortar in the same way as clay bricks.

For very large jobs it is advisable to order ready-mixed concrete, delivered in a truck.

find that river sand is generally clean, and it often contains hard, rounded particles which increase the workability of concrete.

A disadvantage of fines is that the particles have sometimes been washed out by the river water. Beach sand tends to be poorly graded, and usually contains shell particles and salt. If it has been properly washed and graded by the supplier, it may be suitable for building use. Fine, wind-blown sands from desert areas and mine-dump sand (which is also too fine and uniform in particle size) should be avoided. You may find a blended sand which contains some clay, making the mortar easier to work.

Aggregate (crushed stone)

The coarse aggregate which is used to give bulk to concrete may be in the form of gravel, natural pebbles, or crushed stone. Although its properties have less effect on the characteristics of the concrete than do the properties of the sand used, aggregate is usually screened to what is known as single sizes. The most popular size for home improvement projects is ³/₄-inch aggregate. A smaller ¹/₂-inch stone

is easier to work with, but you will need to add more cement to the mixture.

Like sand, aggregate is sold in bags or by volume from builders' suppliers or transportation companies.

Premixed and ready-mixed concrete

Although premixed materials, packaged dry in bags, are suitable only for very small jobs, ready-mixed concrete, delivered by volume in special trucks, is only appropriate for larger projects . However, you can be assured of the exact strength of the concrete as the mixes are determined scientifically.

Lime

Hydrated builder's lime is available at the same outlets that supply cement, loosely bagged sand, and aggregate. It improves the cohesiveness and water-retention qualities of fresh mortar. Lime is sold in 50-pound sacks and is a particularly useful additive if the sand is coarse or lacks very fine particles. Adding lime is also a good precaution to take against the mortar cracking.

Agricultural lime, road lime, and quicklime (calcium oxide) are not suitable for brickwork.

Plasticizer

Plasticizer can be added to mortar to make it more workable, although it has no bonding function. Usually, 2 fl oz of the liquid is added to every 100 pounds of cement, but check the manufacturer's instructions beforehand.

Small quantities of concrete may be mixed on site in a wheelbarrow.

Water

A safe rule of thumb when mixing both concrete and mortar is to use only water which is good enough to drink. If seawater is used, you will find that white powdery deposits tend to form on the surface. If the water is contaminated in any way, with chemicals for instance, this could have an adverse effect on the cement.

Reinforcing

It is unlikely that you will have to reinforce the concrete footings of a garden structure. If you do, you will probably be acting on the advice and specifications of an engineer. Light mesh or a grid of steel rods may be required in the foundation trench, or you may have to set vertical steel bars into the concrete. These will then be built into the wall or pillars.

The most common form of reinforcing incorporated into brickwork itself is a wire mesh available in rolls which is laid over the horizontal plane of every fourth or fifth course. This material is particularly effective for reinforcing the upper surface of small openings left in walls, for example over storage compartments. However, it is no substitute for a lintel.

Lumber

Any wood used for an outdoor project must be sound and durable. Generally, hardwood (from broadleaved trees) is preferable. However some softwoods

Various types of lumber are suitable for garden projects.

(from coniferous trees) are very suitable. In areas where it is available, California redwood is a favorite for use in the garden.

Whatever your choice, make sure that the lumber has been properly processed or pressure-treated with preservatives, preferably at the sawmill. Some types of lumber (in particular teak and balau) will weather well in the open air, but most require some kind of weatherproof sealant to ensure that they will be able to withstand the elements over an extended period of time.

QUANTIFYING AND COSTING

The quantity of materials required will have a direct bearing on the cost of any structure. Of course, if you choose to build one of the designs on pages 52–61, you can simply take the list of materials and work out what these items will cost you. Otherwise you will have to do some mathematical figuring before you start.

The easiest way to cost the materials required to build a structure is to work out exactly how many bricks will be needed, just as we have done on the Plans pages. Once you know this, you

Hoop-iron reinforcing, set in a footing, will help strengthen a pillar.

Steel reinforcing is laid in the foundation trench of a substantial wall.

can establish how much cement, sand, and lime is needed for the mortar. It is a simple matter to determine the materials required for the footings and foundations, provided you have accurate dimensions.

Foundations and footings

The quantities and proportions of the cement, sand, and aggregate required to make concrete for footings depends on the type of structure you are building. The larger it is, in terms of both area and height, the bigger the footings will have to be, and the stronger the concrete mix should be. However, low-strength concrete is quite adequate for the footings of the simple structures featured here. If you are working with $3/4$ inch aggregate, the recommended proportions of cement, sand and crushed stone for hand compaction are 1:4:4. In areas where a good quality gravel is available, the preferred ratio is 1:3:6. If a stronger mix is required, alter these ratios to 1:3:3 (with crushed stone) or 1:2:3 (with gravel).

Local building regulations and codes specify minimum specifications for footings, including the necessary depth below the frostline where relevant. If you are at all uncertain, check these before you start building. As a guide, smaller structures may be built on footings which are between 4 inches and 6 inches thick. Higher, more substantial walls will require a footing of at least 8 inches.

Once you have determined the dimensions relevant to your project, work out the volume of concrete required by multiplying the length x width x thickness or height. If you are using a 1:4:4 mix, you will need 4½–5 bags (495–550 pounds) of cement for every cubic yard; for a 1:2:3 mix you will need eight bags (or 800 pounds) for each cubic yard. Once you know how much cement is required, you can calculate how much sand and aggregate will be needed.

Bricks and blocks

The quickest way to calculate brick quantities is to figure out the total wall area of whatever you are building. For every square yard of half-brick wall you will need 45-50 bricks (depending on their size.) For a one-brick wall you will need to double that number. To work out the number of blocks required, divide the wall area by the area of the side of one block.

When building smaller features, you can also draw the design to scale and establish how many bricks there will be in the first course of each section or side of the structure. Determine the height of the structure and divide this by the height of your bricks, plus a mortar joint. This will give you the number of courses required for the vertical face. Repeat this process for every wall face in the design.

Mortar

When mixing mortar for bricklaying in the ratio 1:4 cement to sand, you can count on using 100 pounds of cement for every 200 bricks laid in a half-brick wall, and the same amount for every 150 laid in a one-brick wall. Mortar works out at about 1 cubic yard per 1,000 bricks. When using larger blocks, the quantities vary. The larger the block, the less cement you will need per square yard. You will need 100 pounds cement to lay a hundred 15½ x 7½ x 7½ inch blocks, and the same amount of cement to lay about fifty 15 x 4 x 4 inch blocks. If you are planning to add lime, add 50 pounds for every 100 pounds of cement.

SETTING OUT

It is absolutely essential to set out the position of any structure correctly. Some helpful pointers are illustrated on page 40, including the useful 3:4:5 method of checking that corners are all kept at 90°. While a builder's square is a reliable guide, it is surprisingly easy to make a mistake and very useful to double-check the layout using this method. Another way to check that the layout is square is to measure diagonally between opposite corners. If you have set out the structure correctly, the two measurements will be the same.

If a structure is to be built on a patio where a slight drainage slope is required, you can set this out with a spirit level, one end of which should be

For your project to run smoothly, it is essential to plan the job and quantify materials carefully.

Use a straightedge to scrape and smooth wet concrete.

Concrete must set thoroughly before bricklaying or paving starts.

set on a small block of wood. The height of the block of wood will depend on the slope required. For a 1:50 slope, which is the minimum requirement, a 2-inch thick block placed under a 80 inch long straightedge will do the trick. Place a spirit level on the straightedge, and position the block under one end of the wood. Then mark the slope with pegs.

If you want to level a slope, the simplest method is with a water level, which consists simply of a length of transparent tubing (or garden hose with a piece of clear tubing pushed into either end.) This homemade tool works on the principle that water finds its own level. Tie one end to a stake and knock this into the ground at the highest point or get a partner to hold it in place. Fill the tube with water before attaching it to a second stake, which should be positioned at the lowest point. Mark off the water level on both stakes, then measure the distance between this mark and the ground at the lowest stake. Then dig out the dirt at the first stake to the same depth.

BUILDING TECHNIQUES

The building techniques required for outdoor brick structures are illustrated in detail on pages 40–51. Once you have familiarized yourself with them and had some practice, you will find that they really are not difficult at all.

Working with concrete

Although the principles of mixing concrete are simple, this can be backbreaking work, especially if you decide to mix by hand yourself. If you are using a reasonable quantity of concrete, it is usually advisable to rent a concrete mixer. You will have to mix it in batches, measuring each one carefully. Use the same container (a large builder's bucket or a clean 25-quart drum) for measuring all the materials.

Mixing

If you are mixing by hand, work on a hard, clean surface. Never mix directly on the ground, as soil can contaminate the concrete and moisture will be absorbed from the mixture. If you mix on asphalt or paving of any sort, hose the area down immediately to prevent the concrete from drying and staining the surface.

First, combine the sand and cement until you get a uniform color, then make a small crater in the center and add water gradually, shoveling the dry materials into the center at the same time. Take care not to add too much water, or you will wash the cement and sand from the heap. When the mix is soft and smooth, rather like heavy cream, you can add the crushed stone or gravel. Some builders prefer to mix all the dry materials first.

When using a concrete mixer, load the coarse aggregate first with a little water and run the machine for a few minutes. This prevents the mix from building up on the blades. Add the sand next, and then the cement.

Placing

It is good building practice to dampen the foundation trench before placing or pouring the concrete, in order to prevent absorption of water from the mix into the soil. Pour the concrete from a wheelbarrow, or shovel it into the trench. Tamp it down with the back of a spade or shovel, then use a straightedge to compact and level it. Start with a chopping motion, then use a sawing movement to finish. Stop when water starts to come to the surface.

Setting and curing

Concrete footings must be left to set, at least overnight, but preferably for several days before building on them. In cold weather, they should be protected from frost by covering them with burlap or plastic. In very hot weather, it is advisable to sprinkle or spray a little water on the surface from time to time to keep it moist.

The hardening of the concrete is the result of a chemical reaction between the cement and water. Although it continues to cure over a period of

A corner block is in place to ensure that bricks are laid correctly.

concrete is clean and has not accumulated sand and garden debris. Use the trowel to place a cylinder of mortar on the foundation and make furrows in it with the pointed tip. Then slide the first brick into position. Now butter the end of your second brick, and slide this into place.

If you watch the professionals at work, you will see that they build up the corners of a wall first, stepping the brickwork back by half a brick at each course. This is known as "racking back" and it helps ensure that the structure is kept square. Use a spirit level (set on a straight-edged length of lumber if it is too short) to check that opposite corners are level. Then string a builder's line between the two corners as a guide to laying the bricks in between. Use a gauge rod to check that each course is equal in height.

years, it gains most of its strength in the first 28 days.

Bricklaying

For anyone planning to do their own bricklaying, the most important tool you will have to learn to use is a bricklayer's trowel. Once you have mastered the technique of buttering the ends and sides of bricks with the trowel, you will be able to workquickly. The other vital aspect is to ensure that each and every brick you lay is level and plumb.

A spirit level will enable you to do this, just make certain that the bubble in the vial is always centered.

The mortar for bricklaying is mixed in exactly the same way as concrete, except that aggregate is not added. If lime is used, add this with the cement and sand.

Once you know which bond you are going to use (see pages 31–32), you can get started. The first course is laid on mortar set on the concrete foundation. Make sure that the

Rendering

If you are not using facebricks, you will probably want to render the surface once the brickwork is complete. Mortar is used, usually mixed in the same ratio as the bricklaying mortar, so that the two are compatible. To make the mortar more pliable, plasticizer or lime is usually added to the mixture. The

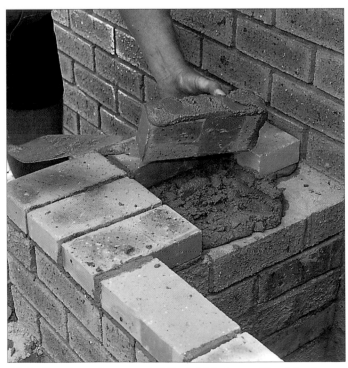

"Butter" mortar onto one end of the brick before putting it in place.

A metal pointing tool is used to scrape out the joints of brickwork.

addition of a bonding agent will also help the mortar stick to the surface.

If the brick surface absorbs too much water from the fresh render, the mortar will be weakened. Spray some water evenly over the brickwork the day before you are going to start work. If it has been raining, allow the walls to become surface-dry before applying the mortar. Remember that cracking is more likely if the mortar is applied in hot sun or strong wind conditions.

Once the mixture is ready, apply it to the surface using a rectangular plasterer's trowel. Press it down firmly to ensure good adhesion. It needs to set for about an hour before you can scrape the surface with a straightedge or a screed board. Once you have a reasonably level surface, smooth it out further with a wooden float to get a really smooth finish.

Mortar used to render walls must not be allowed to dry out too quickly, otherwise it will not cure properly and it may crack. To prevent this, dampen the surface by hosing with a gentle spray several times a day over a two- or three-day period. It is important to ensure that the spray is really fine, otherwise it could damage the finish.

Paved surfaces

If worktops and garden tables are to be paved, you will usually lay the

A normal mortar mix is used to render brickwork which is to be painted.

pavers in mortar in exactly the same way as any other bricks or blocks. On the other hand, when paving the fire-bed of a barbecue structure, it is best to lay the pavers on sand, and to butt them up against one another

in order to form a solid base for the fire. Remember that clay bricks are fired at very high temperatures and will not be damaged by the fire. However, a mortar or plain concrete base will tend to crack.

USEFUL TERMS

Aggregate Although sand is the fine aggregate added to both mortar and concrete, this term is also used to described the gravel added to concrete. This may be gravel or crushed stone, depending on what is available in your location.

Bond The arrangement of bricks to ensure that they overlap and therefore bind together to form a solid, stable mass. Various patterns may be formed, some of which, if laid in facebrick, can create a decorative effect.

Buttering Method used to apply mortar to the ends or sides of bricks during the bricklaying process.

Course A complete row of laid bricks.

Several courses form a wall or part of another brick structure.

Excavation The foundation trench.

Footing Projecting concrete course at the foot of a wall, pillar, or pier.

Foundation The concrete base on which brickwork rests.

Frog Indented side of a brick.

Jointing Method used to finish off and neaten the joints in brickwork when facebricks have been used.

Lap The amount a brick overlaps the bricks in the course below.

Header The short end of a brick. A header course features the end of the brick on the outside of the wall.

Perpend The vertical joints in brickwork.

Pointing The process of filling in brick or block joints with mortar.

Racking back Method of building up the brickwork at the corners and ends of walls.

Reinforcing rod Metal mesh or rod built into concrete and brickwork to strengthen it. They also help tie the wall to the earth in a retaining wall.

Stretcher The long side or face of a brick; hence stretcher bond (running bond.) A stretcher course features the long side of the brick on the outside of the wall.

Weep holes Unmortared joints left near the base of walls or planters for drainage. This also keeps excess water pressure from building up behind the wall.

STEP-BY-STEP BUILDING METHODS

In the following pages, important building principles and basic bricklaying techniques are outlined, along with a description of the materials and tools you will need to build a brick structure in your garden. These step-by-step instructions show how to employ the various skills, starting with a section which illustrates clearly how to set out any project. To make the building process more realistic, step-by-step photographs show several specific brick features under construction.

One series of pictures follows the construction of a simple barbecue unit which incorporates a very basic storage area.

The second shows how seating, tables, planters, and a storage box are assembled. These structures are not presented as projects, and no materials lists are given. Instead, the focus is on the procedures followed and techniques used. Once you have mastered them, you should be able to tackle any outdoor brick project.

You will see how the principles previously explained are put into practice, how single and double walls are built, corners constructed, and pillars incorporated into a design. You will also see how various tools are used. Formwork is used to create a working surface alongside the fire-bed of a barbecue, and the same project also demonstrates how to create an opening in any brick structure. Weep holes are left in planters, illustrating a simple drainage method.

BUILDING METHODS: SETTING OUT

The first step in any outdoor building project is to set out the site correctly. You will need to decide exactly where the structure is to be located, according to the dimensions and layout of your plan, and then you will have to mark it out, clearly showing where foundation trenches must be dug. The foundations are always slightly larger than the structure itself, an important point to remember when setting out.

One of the advantages of building smaller garden features is that, because of their size, it is usually easy to double-check the layout. A good way to do this is to lay out loose bricks to check the area to be excavated and ensure that the design will fit the area intended for construction.

If there is a problem, it is much easier to sort it out now than when the bricks have been mortared.

Most structures tackled by home improvement builders are square or rectangular in shape, so all the angles where walls meet one another will be 90°. Occasionally, a design may feature acute or obtuse angles or curved lines.

The simplest way to check that corners are square (or at 90°) is to use the 3:4:5 method. What this means is that the length of the shortest side of the triangle must be equal to three units of measurement, the adjacent short side must be four, and the line which joins the two ends must be five units in length. If the structure is large enough, these may

be units of 3 yards, 4 yards, and 5 yards respectively. A much smaller unit may be 1-foot, 2-foot, and 3-foot units. Any other multiples will also work, for instance 30 inches, 40 inches, and 50 inches.

You can set out a circular structure by making a basic compass with pegs and string. Knock one peg into the central point, attach a string to it, and then rotate the string, marking a ring of points around the circumference. The most important thing to remember is that the length of the string must equal the radius of your circle.

Once the layout has been pegged, mark the position of the foundations or footings with dry cement, lime, chalk, or even flour. Flour is the least expensive and sometimes the handiest option.

Use the 3:4:5 method to check for square.

Use a peg and string to lay out circles.

Check your layout with loose bricks.

BARBECUE

Anyone who wants to build a simple brick barbecue in the garden or on a patio will find these step-by-step instructions invaluable. It does not matter whether you want to copy the design, adapt it, or simply to use the various basic building skills which are illustrated. This helpful guide will enable you to create a special structure of which you can be proud.

Various elements are covered, from foundation to finishes. The aim is to give a broad indication of what is involved when building a structure to be used for cooking and storage. The inclusion of a solid, paved worktop will increase the versatility of the design.

The fire-bed featured here is sunken, and surrounded by brickwork on three sides. This means there is no need to use formwork or any other kind of reinforcing to create the cooking surface. Instead, a basic brick box is constructed and filled with dirt removed from the foundation trenches. This is then compacted, topped with sand, and paved with clay bricks.

Since many barbecue designs feature a storage area for firewood, coal, and other items below the cooking area, the step-by-step project also includes instructions which will enable you to tackle this design variation. The upper surface of the storage area forms a preparation table for food which is to be cooked on the barbecue or for serving, and a similar surface may be built as the fire-bed itself. In this event, the most important element is the formwork which is provided to support the surface during construction.

If a chimney of some kind is to be built, formwork will also be necessary to support the front wall. Although the central cavity will be left open, the essential principles are the same.

This particular barbecue design measures 74 x 28½ inches and is 38 inches above the ground. The large fire surface has dimensions based on the average metal oil-drum, which is often cut in half lengthwise for use by the outdoor cook. A 36 x 24-inch gridiron will slot in and cover the area.

MATERIALS

Facebricks are used for building because they are a low-maintenance option for any structure which is to be used for cooking. Matching paving bricks are laid in the fire-bed, forming the exposed working surface, and they are also used to finish the inside of the storage compartment.

If you decide to follow the design exactly, you will need 270 facebricks and 58 matching pavers (not allowing for wastage.)

The formwork used here is permanent, but it is not intended to be seen after completion of the structure. For this reason, relatively thin ¼ inch x 16 inch wide fibercement boards are placed over the opening to cover it. Once the surface is paved, this material is not visible. Any other slim board (or even metal) may be used, but it should be weatherproof. Concrete cast in situ and concrete lintels are not suitable.

FOUNDATIONS

As this is not a heavy structure, a foundation of 4–6 inches is ample. Use a 1:4:4 or 1:3:6 concrete mix, depending on soil conditions and the gravel available in your area.

When laying out the structure (see facing page), make sure that the foundations are about 4 inches wider than the brickwork on all sides. If the structure is to be built alongside paving laid previously, the foundation may be flush with the existing bricks.

1 Decide where the barbecue structure is to be located and peg it out with string as described on page 40. Make sure that all the measurements are accurate, and use a steel builder's square to ensure that the corners are at right angles.

2 The area pegged out here is adjacent to existing paving and measures 82 x 32½ inches. You can remove the pegs and string before you dig the foundations, provided that you first mark the outline of the proposed trench with chalk, cement, or flour.

3 If the area where you are building is grassed you may be able to use the grass elsewhere in the garden. Use the sharp end of a spade to cut into the turf, then dig out the sods neatly and carefully. Reserve any excess dirt.

4 Bricks placed on edge are useful to indicate the upper level of your concrete. Place a spirit level across the bricks and check that the base of the trench is level. If you want a deeper foundation, use pegs marked to the correct height.

5 Now mix concrete following the instructions given on page 37. Moisten the soil in the trench to prevent the water from the fresh mix from being absorbed into the ground. Transport the mixture in a wheelbarrow and tip it out into the trench.

6 The concrete should be level with the top of the bricks (or pegs.) Level it off roughly with the back of your spade or shovel, and then neaten with a 2x4, using a sawing movement. Use a chopping motion to compact.

7 Once the concrete has set, lay out the bricks without mortar, positioning them correctly on the slab. Now is the time to make any minor alterations, for instance if you are not happy with the design or find that too many half-bricks are needed.

8 Use a square to check that all four corners of the proposed structure are at 90°. Use a pencil or chalk to mark the position of the bricks on the concrete. Although you will have to recheck the angles later, this helps to ensure accuracy.

9 Mix mortar in the ratio 1:4 (cement: sand), adding lime or plasticizer if required. Lay a strip of mortar 4–6 inches thick where the first brick is to be laid. Use the tip of your trowel to make a jagged furrow along the center of the strip.

10 Now you can bed the first brick in mortar. If it has obliterated the line you made on the concrete, use a steel square and the tip of the trowel to mark exactly where the brick should be positioned. Press the brick firmly into place and tap with the trowel.

11 It is essential that the first brick is flat and level, as you will use this surface to gauge the alignment of other bricks. Set the spirit level across the brick and check that the bubble in the vial is centered, tapping lightly with the handle of the trowel if it is not.

12 Check again with the spirit level, this time along the length of the brick. If the bubble in the vial is not centered, tap the brick gently with the trowel handle. Alternatively, remove a little of the mortar from underneath the brick and check again.

13 Once the first brick is in place, you can butter one end of each consecutive brick to be laid. Trowel on a wedge of mortar and spread it across the end. Then use the pointed tip of your bricklaying trowel to make furrows to aid bonding.

14 Put a little more mortar onto the slab, at right angles to the first brick you laid, and create a furrow in it as before. Slide the second brick into place, allowing the mortar on the end to form a joint. Push it firmly into the mortar and tap with the trowel handle.

15 You will not be able to tell whether or not it is perfectly level unless you use the correct tools. Place the spirit level across the upper surface of the two bricks and continue tapping gently with the trowel until the bubble is centered.

16 It is essential that all the corners of the structure are at right angles. Even if you have followed all the previous guidelines, use a steel builder's square to check the angle again now, before the mortar sets. Then lay your next brick.

17 You can lay the first course of the side wall, but do not lay the front wall until the first corner has been built up. This is the best way to ensure that the structure will be straight and square. Put mortar on the trowel and smooth it onto the bricks.

18 Lay the first brick of the second course at the corner, pushing it firmly into the furrowed mortar. Use the spirit level frequently to check that the upper surface is flat. As you work, make sure that the textured face of each brick facing outward.

19 The surface which will form the outside walls must also be flat and plumb. Do not forget to use the spirit level vertically to ensure that the ends of the bricks are properly aligned. Tap the first brick in the second course outward if it is not in line vertically.

20 Continue to build up the corner, checking all surfaces regularly. Even if both horizontal and vertical surfaces are flat, level, and plumb, it pays to double-check across the diagonal. You can use a straightedge of any sort to do this.

21 The side walls are only three bricks long. Leave the middle brick out of the second course and lay a brick at the corner of the back wall. Check from corner to corner, across the full length of this section of wall, before filling in to complete the course.

22 Scrape any excess mortar off the bricks with the trowel as you work. When using facebricks, it is much easier to keep the surface clean than to try to remove surplus mortar at a later stage. Do not waste what is scraped off, you can use all of it.

23 Even though you are buttering the end of the bricks, you will find that there are a few gaps in the joints which need to be filled as you work. Lift a little of the mortar onto the trowel, and, using a chopping movement, point (or fill) these joints.

24 Now you can move to the opposite side of the structure and lay the first course at the corner. Once a few of the bricks are in place, string a line between the two corners, making certain that it is level with the upper surface of the bricks.

25 Then lay the course of bricks which will form the front wall of the barbecue and contain the fire-bed. The line you have set up will enable you to make certain that it is absolutely straight. Take care not to let any of the bricks touch it and push it out of place.

26 Continue building up the walls, using the bricks at each corner as a guide. If they are level with each other, you will find it easier to ensure that the course as a whole is level. It pays to be meticulous. Tap any uneven bricks with the trowel handle.

27 Once you have laid the first couple of courses at the front of the structure, lay the internal walls which will divide the cooking surface from the storage area. The position of these walls will depend upon the design of your barbecue.

28 This design features a relatively wide fire-bed, with storage space on one side only. A double brick wall on the other side provides a narrow serving area and will enable you to step the brickwork so that it provides a support for the grid.

29 Decide on the best position for the cooking grid. You will need to support it with metal (inserted into the mortar during bricklaying), or by stepping the brickwork. Lay the bricks at this level slightly off the edge of the wall below, so forming a narrow shelf.

30 Lay the bricks in the same way for the outside wall. This will result in a thicker mortar joint at this level, but it will not be obvious in the overall effect. The overlap should be equal on both sides, and just wide enough to support the grid.

31 Use a long spirit level to check that the bricks are level. If your spirit level is too short to span the gap, set it on a 2x4. Do not rely on your own judgement. If the bricks are not level the gridiron will wobble and shake, as it will be unstable.

32 Now complete the brickwork, continually checking both the horizontal and vertical surfaces. Here, the front wall is built up two courses for the storage area and seven for the fire-bed. You may also create a second step for the grid if you wish.

33 Once most of the brickwork is complete, but before you lay the pavers on the upper surface, fill the central cavity with broken bricks, crushed stone, or sand. You can also use the soil which was excavated from the foundation trench.

34 Use a punner or solid pole to compact the fill in layers and make certain there are no air-pockets. This is especially important if you are using rubble which is not regular in shape and size. Hosing the fill gently with water also aids compaction.

35 Cut the formwork to size. Here, 6-inch wide lengths of fibercement are abutted to form a solid surface which will support the paving bricks. Brace the formwork from underneath with lumber. This can be removed once the mortar has set.

36 Matching pavers may now be laid in mortar, over the formwork, to create a serving or working surface. Lay the first two at opposite corners and use the spirit level to check that they are level with one another before laying the balance.

37 Lay pavers over the entire upper surface. allowing those along the back wall to form a slight, decorative lip if you wish. Butter the ends of the bricks and use a trowel to fill in any open joints. Use a jointing tool to neaten the joints.

38 The pavers which are to form the fire bed are laid on sand rather than in mortar. Shovel a 1-inch layer of soft building sand over the fill, then smooth and level it with a 2x4. Abut the bricks and use a rubber mallet to level them.

39 Use mortar to fill in around the edges of the pavers and keep them in place. Brush sand over the surface so that it fills the joints. Finally, use a piece of metal to rake out any excess mortar from the joints in the walls to give a nice, clean finish.

Brick features may be built as individual units or as part of a more elaborate plan. These step-by-step instructions will enable you to do either. You can copy the versatile design shown here, which incorporates ample seating, storage, built-in table tops, and stepped planters, or construct any one of these features on its own. Alternatively, you can use the ideas and techniques demonstrated here to create your own design.

For those wanting to duplicate the design, the layout includes a 152-inch long, 14¼-inch wide, half-brick wall which has three supporting 14 x 14-inch piers. This was built to shield a driveway from view and at the same time add privacy to the area. It is also used as the backrest to the bench which is set in front of it. The seat itself is constructed with six lengths of 3-inch wide lumber which rest on three supporting piers, built to five courses above what will be the finished floor surface of the patio.

Tables are incorporated at both ends of the 92-inch long bench. One measures 18 x 18 inches, while the other is only 18 x 8¾ inches, but is quite adequate for drinks and dishes. Two planters, built to different heights

(one three courses high and the other five courses) are built at one end of the bench. The inside measurements of these are about 22¼ x 8¾ inches and 18 x 8¾ inches respectively. The storage box, which doubles as a second seating structure, is slightly wider than the bench (60 x 28 inches), so that it can be used to store pillows and other bulky items. The lid is made from exterior plywood and planks and is hinged to an existing wall.

Since structures may be built on both strip and slab foundations (see page 36), both types are illustrated, along with an invaluable hint on how to provide essential drainage in the base of a brick planter.

Most of the brickwork involves building single (or half-brick) walls, although construction of the central pier supporting the bench shows how the thicker one-brick wall is built.

MATERIALS

Although facebricks are used to construct all of these features, part of the planter walls is rendered to blend in with the exterior of the house. The tables and upper edges of the planters are topped with matching paving bricks, providing a smooth and

attractive surface. If you decide to copy the design, you will need about 300 facebricks and 13 pavers for the bench, storage box, tables, and planters. An additional 300 will be required to build the 6-foot high wall.

Various types of lumber may be used for the seats, although you must be sure that it is suitable for outdoor use and will withstand weathering. All types should be treated against infestation and sealed in some way (see page 35).

The interior walls of the planters are sealed with a bitumen-based product to prevent future discoloration caused by constant moisture.

FOUNDATIONS

Relatively small, 4–6-inch thick foundations are quite adequate for the smaller features. Foundations for the wall should be thicker (at least 8 inches thick.) Check whether your local building codes contain minimum requirements or zoning guidelines for your location.

When mixing the concrete, use a 1:4:4 or 1:3:6 concrete mix, depending on soil conditions and the type of gravel available in your area.

1 Use a retractable steel tape measure and a builder's square to set out the foundation trenches as described on page 40. Make sure that they are about 4 inches wider on all sides than the structure itself. Peg out the area with long nails and string.

2 Before you begin to excavate the foundation trenches, mark the area pegged out with chalk, lime, cement, or flour. Then remove the nails (or pegs) and string. This shows the layout of the screen wall and three supporting piers.

3 Dig the foundation trench for the wall and piers to a depth of at least 8 inches. Remove all vegetation and keep the ground surface as flat and even as you can, as this will enable you to cast an even slab to support the brickwork.

4 Mark out and dig the rest of the trenches to a depth of 6 inches. Strip foundations may be laid for the storage box structure, rather than throwing a solid slab. Make sure these are at least 4–8 inches wider than the walls will be.

5 Use a 2x4 set on bricks, together with a spirit level, to determine where the upper surface of the concrete will be. The bricks are then left in position, as a permanent and failsafe guide. There is no need to remove them from the trench.

6 When all the trenches have been dug and leveled, mix concrete as described on page 37, and carry it in a wheelbarrow. To prevent water from being drawn out of the fresh concrete, moisten the soil before shoveling the concrete into place.

7 If you need to step the concrete slightly at any point, use loosely laid bricks to hold the wet mixture in place while it sets. Here the bench and table foundation is higher than that cast for the wall and piers. Compact and level the concrete thoroughly.

8 When building planters, it is vital to provide drainage of some sort. A simple solution is to position several bricks at the base of the structure before placing the concrete. For larger planters, simply throw strip foundations, leaving the center open.

9 When the concrete has set, but is not yet hard, remove the bricks. If you leave them for too long, you will have to chip them out with a chisel. To prevent this problem, gently shake the bricks from time to time while the concrete is setting.

10 Remove the bricks used to step the foundation and leave the concrete to set thoroughly, at least overnight. Before you start laying the bricks, set them out on the foundations, without any mortar, to check the layout you have planned.

11 This shows the position of the central pier which will support the lumber used to create seating. Because it is stepped above the first course of the wall, one extra brick will be needed alongside the wall to support it.

12 A section of the wall is included in the design at one end. If you are not building a screen wall, the back of the structure will simply be lower, in keeping with height of the planters and table, and the pier will not be included.

13 The storage box and adjacent table area are set out against an existing wall and pillar. Each site will differ and there is no reason that these features should not be freestanding. Alternatively, you could build a low wall behind the box to form a backrest.

14 Mark the position of the loose bricks with chalk or pencil, then remove them. Mix mortar in the required ratio and start laying the bricks at any of the corners, as described in steps 9–16 on page 42. Make sure the first brick is level.

15 The first course must also be square. Use the correct tools to check the angles and to make absolutely sure that the upper surface of the first course is flat and level. To do this, set the spirit level at various angles along the tops of the bricks.

16 Do not assume that any existing walls or features are square and plumb. Rather check your own brickwork regularly. If the walls of this storage box are not laid accurately, you will have problems fitting the lid at a later stage.

17 There are various ways to build pillars and piers. This 14 x 14-inch pillar is constructed with four bricks, so that it can bond with the half-brick wall. Lay the first course of bricks on a bed of mortar and use a spirit level to check that they are flat.

18 You can leave the central core hollow, or, if the pillar is relatively high, insert a reinforcing rod through the center and fill the hollow with mortar or a weak concrete mix, This pillar is built with a half-brick in the center, making it reasonably solid.

19 Make sure that the brickwork is square before you go any further. Here, the wall continues from the pillar. This will ensure that the bricks bond well, but the effect of a running stretcher bond will be interrupted by a half brick at times.

20 Continue to lay the first course of all the features. The configuration of the table follows a paving stack bond at this stage. The next course will be laid so that all the bricks in this part of the structure bond properly and do not fall over.

21 Once the first course of bricks is in place, you can start laying the next course, preferably at a corner. If there is a wide expanse of wall, use a spirit level to align this first, and then use it as a reference point for the rest of brickwork at this level.

22 Then move to the next corner. Align the two outside bricks, and string a builder's line at the correct height. Then lay bricks between the corners to complete the course. Be sure to bond the bricks to form a half-brick wall in stretcher bond.

23 When you lay the second course of the table adjoining the planters, you will need to cut some of the bricks to ensure the structure is properly bonded. You cannot just lay them in the opposite direction as there will be a gap through the middle.

24 The central pier which will form a support for the bench must also be built using stretcher bond, even though this little wall is only five courses high. Lay the first brick of the second course across the front of the two parallel bricks in the first course.

25 Knock the bricks into place with the handle of the trowel and then check the corners again with the builder's square. Use the spirit level to make sure the brickwork at each end is properly aligned with the central pier. It will be difficult to rectify faults later.

26 It is important to create weepholes at the base of the wall to allow water to drain from the patio. The simplest method is to leave some of the vertical joints unmortared. These holes will be just above ground level once paving is laid.

27 Use a pin and builder's line to keep the courses straight. Push the pin into the wet mortar one course below the one you are laying, and pull the line around the corner at an angle. Wind the line around a loose brick to keep it in place at the other end.

28 Even if you are buttering one end of each brick (see step 13 on page 43), you will find that you need to add mortar to some of the joints. Put a little mortar on the trowel and cut gently into the joint with the edge of the tool, tapping it slightly.

29 The stepped planters are built up three and five courses above the eventual level of the paved patio. The supporting pier for the bench is one course lower than the table surface which is incorporated alongside the two planters.

30 When creating a solid brick surface, a good tip from the professionals is to lay the outside bricks before filling in the center. This helps to keep the vertical surfaces plumb. Take care not to shift the outer bricks when you lay those in the middle.

31 Follow the same procedure when building the larger table adjacent to the wall at the other end. Make sure that each course bonds with the one beneath it, and finish the table area one course higher than the supporting pier for the bench.

32 Continue building the screen wall to the required height. You will need to string a line along the entire length of the wall to keep the brick courses straight. It is a good idea to use a gauge rod now and then to check that all the joints are even.

33 If any part of the brickwork is to be rendered, this can be done once the mortar used to lay the bricks has set. Mix a new batch of mortar and lay it onto your surface with a plasterer's trowel, applying enough pressure to make it stick to the bricks.

34 The render should be between 4 and 6 inches thick. Leave it while it begins to set, then, after about an hour, use a 2x4 or a spirit level to scrape and smooth the surface. Accuracy is not important in this particular case.

35 Once the surface is reasonably smooth, use a wooden float to create a more even finish. Use an even pressure and a regular wrist movement, but do not over-trowel or the finer material will come to the surface and may cause cracking.

36 The next step is to finish table tops and all other exposed horizontal brick surfaces with pavers. Where the rendered surface meets a facebrick wall, you should use the spirit level to ensure that the pavers are level on the vertical plane.

37 Once the first paver is in position, you can lay the rest of the bricks around the lip of the higher planter and on the surface of the smaller table top. Bed the pavers in mortar and butter one side and one end before pushing into place.

38 Then lay paving bricks around the top of the lower planter, first filling in any holes with mortar. Place a cylinder of mortar on the upper surface and create a slight furrow with the trowel in exactly the same way as you would to lay ordinary bricks.

39 Place the first paving brick in position and check that it is level. Butter the end of the second paver and push it into place. Then use your spirit level again, and tap any uneven bricks with a rubber mallet until they are absolutely flat and level.

40 When you have completed the planters and the mortar is well set, paint a bitumen-based sealant on the inside surface. This will prevent moisture from affecting the outer skin of the brickwork. When the bitumen is dry, fill the box with soil and plant it.

41 When finishing off the table top positioned in the corner between old and new walls, lay the first brick at the outer corner and ensure that both the horizontal and the vertical surfaces are plumb. Make sure that the joints are clean and tidy.

42 Place an even bed of mortar on the upper surface of the brickwork. Then butter the sides of the bricks as you lay the outer row. Knock each one gently into place with a mallet and check that they are all level with one another.

43 Butter both the length and the top of each of the bricks laid on the inner row of the table top. There will be a slight gap between the edge of the pavers and the wall. This can be filled with mortar, using a trowel to make sure that it is level with the pavers.

44 Once the table top is complete, you may find that some of the joints need to be filled (or pointed). It will also be necessary to neaten the joints with a special trowel or jointer. Those without specialist tools could use a piece of metal instead.

45 Make the seat for the bench by screwing four 18 x 2½ x 1¾ inch wide slats across six 1-inch lengths. Position them so that there is one short piece on either side of the central brick pier, and one on the inside of each of the end piers.

46 The back rest is made with four 2¾-inch wide lengths of lumber which are screwed to the wall. This will prevent a textured facebrick finish from scraping against you or damaging clothing. It also creates the impression of more substantial built-in furniture.

47 Make the storage box lid from a 60 x 28½ sheet of exterior plywood and nine 60 x 2¾ inch wide slats. Cut five shallow channels across the width of the slats. Glue them to one side of the plywood then, working from the other side, tack the slats down.

48 Glue and screw four slats, 28 inches long and 1¼ inches thick, across the board, using 2-inch long screws to secure each of the nine seating slats. Screw brass hinges to the lid, then attach it to the wall with screws and fiber or plastic anchors.

DESIGNS AND PLANS

An attractive and useful storage box with a hinged lid doubles as a bench on a compact but much-used patio. Large enough to house pillows and other bulky items which might be damaged by rain, it is built on a solid concrete slab, and against an existing wall, which is not shown on the illustration. You will require an additional 39 bricks as well as an extra 25 pounds of cement and sand for mortar if you need to construct the back wall of a freestanding storage box. Facebricks should be used to build the basic structure, while any good quality lumber recommended for exterior use may be used for the lid.

If a soft wood such as pine) is chosen, it may be necessary to use thicker slats to prevent any possible buckling.

MATERIALS

Foundation
66 pounds cement
270 pounds sand
1270 pounds stone

Brickwork
72 facebricks
(+ 39 if required)
55 pounds cement
(+ 25 pounds extra, if required)
28 pounds lime (optional)
220 pounds sand (+ 25 pounds extra, if required)

Lid
60 x 28 x 2 inch sheet exterior-grade plywood
9 x 60 x 2³/₄ x 1³/₄ inch slats
4 x 28 x 28 inch x 8 inch crosspieces
6-inch panel pins
36 x 2-inch brass screws
2 brass butt-hinges with brass screws and expandable anchors
waterproof wood-glue

28 in

60 in

1 Measure and mark a 64 x 32-inch area for the foundation. Dig to a depth of 4 inches, compact, and level the ground.
2 Mix the concrete and place over the foundation area. Allow to set overnight.
3 Lay the brick walls of the box, using stretcher bond. Allow the mortar to set thoroughly.
4 Meanwhile, assemble the lid. First cut five shallow channels across the width of each of the 60-inch slats to aid drainage. Then position these lengths, with the grooves facing upward, on a solid surface so that you have 12-inch

gaps between each. Glue and tack the plywood on top, using a good quality waterproof wood-glue and casing nails. When the glue is dry, position the four 28-inch crosspieces evenly across the ply, so that those at each end are flush with the edges. Glue and then screw through the lumber to secure the slats.
5 When the glue is completely dry and the mortar thoroughly set, screw the hinges to the lid and then affix to the wall using screws and expandable anchors.

Simple yet good-looking, and easy-to-build, this raised and freestanding planter will add visual interest to any patio. Furthermore, its dimensions are easily altered and it could be increased in size to suit the style and shape of your paved outdoor area. Although this planter can be built on a strip foundation, it is simpler to throw a slab, placing bricks on the ground and then removing them to create instant drainage holes, once the concrete has almost set. With a structure this size, wastage of concrete is minimal. If you are building on an existing patio, you will need to chop out some of the bricks to enable water to drain away.

MATERIALS

Foundation
44 pounds cement
88 pounds sand
88 pounds stone

Brickwork
66 facebricks
11 paving bricks
44 pounds cement
25 pounds lime (optional)
176 pounds sand

1 Measure out an area 32 x 40 inches and peg it out. Dig a 4-inch deep foundation.

2 Mix the concrete and, before laying, set two or three bricks in the center of the proposed structure. Lay the slab and allow the concrete to set. Before it becomes totally hard, remove the bricks.

3 Start laying the bricks using stretcher bond. Create weepholes in the second course by excluding every second vertical joint. Piping can be inserted if more substantial drainage is required.

4 Lay as many courses as required and top with a final course of pavers.

5 If you wish, seal the interior walls of the planter with a bitumen-based product to prevent future discoloration of the bricks by constant moisture.

27 3/8 in

32 in

Delightfully rustic seating alongside the house not only provides a resting place, but also adds character to the plain wall. Simple to build, this is a perfect weekend project for the home handyman. These two seats are built of facebrick, but the same design could be rendered and painted. Although quantities specified call for a solid concrete core in each seat, you can save on materials by filling the central gap with sand to about the height of the fourth brick course, compacting well, and then topping with concrete.

MATERIALS

Foundations
44 pounds cement
176 pounds sand
176 pounds stone

Brickwork
60 bricks
33 pounds cement
16½ pounds lime (optional)
132 pounds sand

Woodwork
6 x 5 x 9 x 20 inch
   lumber for seats
6 x 3 x ¾ inch
   x 20 inch lumber
   for back rests
36 x 1¾ inch brass screws
   with expandable anchors

1 Measure out the two seats and peg the area required for foundations. Dig to a depth of 14 inches.
2 Mix half the concrete and lay the slab. Allow to set thoroughly overnight.
3 Build the base plinth using stretcher bond. Leave until the mortar has set.
4 Mix a new batch of concrete and place in the center of the brickwork. Compact well and level the upper surface.
5 When the concrete is well set, screw the seat lumber to the side walls, using two screws at the ends of each board.
6 Screw the narrow back rest boards to the adjacent wall, ensuring they are evenly spaced.

18 in
18 in

An attractive corner planter not only adds interest to the wall, giving it a more professional finish, but it also allows for visual access, which is particularly important at busy intersections. Built with precast concrete blocks, this design is part of a rendered wall and most appropriate if used around the boundary of a lot. As the structure is outside the garden itself, it is advisable to choose shrubs and plants which will not demand much maintenance. Materials specified will allow you to build the wall and planter plus about140 inches of wall on either side.

MATERIALS

Foundations
704 pounds cement
40 cu. inches sand
40 cu. inches stone

Blockwork
408 x 15$\frac{1}{2}$ x 7$\frac{3}{4}$ x 7$\frac{3}{4}$ inch concrete
   blocks, about 40 halved and broken
297 pounds cement
150 pounds lime (optional)
297 pounds sand

Mortar for rendering
320 kg cement
160 kg lime (optional)
1.6 m³ sand

1 Mark out the position of the wall and planter as illustrated, leaving the base of the planter untouched.
2 Dig the foundation trenches to at least 10 inches.
3 Mix the concrete with water in a cement: sand: stone ratio of 1:4:4 and place in the trenches. Compact, level, and leave to set overnight.
4 Build the wall and planter using stretcher bond. The planter should be four courses high and the wall itself 12 courses.

5 Use half-blocks and broken pieces to build the capping along the top.
6 Once the mortar has set, render the wall, and finish off the capping to create a neat, sloping finish as illustrated.
7 When the mortar has set and is completely dry, paint the wall.

140 in   140 in

88 in

This practical screen wall is built on a curve to add character to a patio or utility area. The adjacent seat, which curves alongside the wall, may be used as a resting spot or to display pot plants. Although this design has been roughly bagged with cement to give it a rustic feel, it could also be rendered for a more formal effect, or built with facebricks to match the walls of the house. The seat has been topped with tiles as an elegant finish. If facebricks are used for construction, a paving-brick topping might be a good idea. The materials listed will allow you to build the seat and a 48-inch high wall which is about 128 inches long.

MATERIALS

Foundations
154 pounds cement
616 pounds sand
616 pounds stone

Brickwork
437 bricks
24 brick-sized tiles
   (or paving bricks)
330 pounds cement
165 pounds lime (optional)
1320 pounds sand

1 Measure the line the wall will follow and peg out the foundations as shown on the illustration. Measure and peg out the area required for the adjacent seat. Dig to a depth of 10 inches. Compact and level the earth.
2 Mix the concrete and lay the foundation for both wall and seat. Allow the concrete to set before continuing with the brickwork.
3 Lay the bricks for the one-brick wall first, using an English

bond with alternate courses of headers and stretchers. Then lay the bricks for the seat. Allow the mortar to set.
4 If desired, mix a small amount of mortar, adding more water than usual, and smear the mixture onto the wall with burlap to achieve a thin, "bagged" finish.
5 Once all the mortar has set thoroughly, top the seat with tiles as illustrated, cutting those at the back to fit. Paint the structure.

13³/4 inches

72 in

An elegant, period-style bench can be constructed in the garden by anyone who has basic bricklaying skills. Smoothly rendered with a mortar mix and then painted, it will soon look like a beautifully sculpted piece of garden furniture. This design is built with ordinary bricks, using simple stretcher bond. The central cavity, which forms the seat of the structure, may be filled with rubble, even though materials here call for sand. Whatever material is used must be well compacted before being topped with a layer of concrete, which is skimmed with mortar to create a smooth finish.

MATERIALS

Foundations
220 pounds cement
892 pounds sand
892 pounds stone

Brickwork
207 bricks
110 pounds cement
25 kg lime (optional)
200 kg sand

Mortar for rendering
44 pounds cement
22 pounds lime (optional)
176 pounds sand

Seating slab
24 cu. inches sand or fill
33 pounds cement
132 pounds sand
132 pounds stone

1 Choose the position of the seat and peg out a rectangle 88 x 48 inches. Excavate to a depth of about 6 inches.
2 Mix the concrete in the ratio 1:4:4 and then lay to create a slab foundation. Allow to set thoroughly – at least overnight.
3 Build the walls to form the basic structure of the seat, as illustrated.
4 When the mortar has set, fill the central cavity with sand or fill. Compact well.
5 Mix the concrete for the seating slab and lay it over the compacted sand. Leave to set thoroughly.
6 Finally, render the outside walls of the structure with a 1:4 mortar mix, filling in all gaps between the bricks.

36³/₄ in

80 in

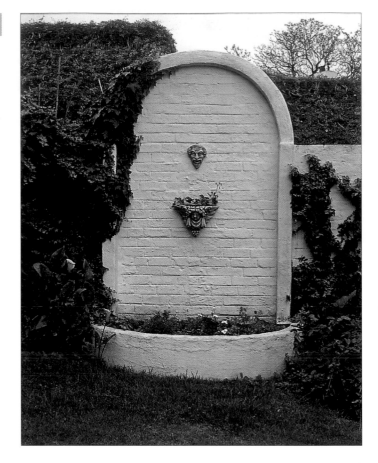

This unusual arched planter has been built as a feature in a 106-inch high garden boundary wall. While the central panel has simply been lightly bagged with a cement/sand slush, the curved wall and surrounding trim have been neatly rendered for effect. Decorated with a precast gargoyle and bowl, and planted with colorful annuals, this design will brighten a dull spot in any garden, large or small. If built on a solid concrete slab and properly waterproofed, it could even be adapted as a pond. Quantities specified do not include brickwork for the adjacent wall or its foundations.

MATERIALS

Foundation
110 pounds cement
440 pounds sand
440 pounds stone

Render
44 pounds cement
22 pounds lime (optional)
176 pounds sand

Brickwork
345 bricks
198 pounds cement
99 pounds lime (optional)
792 pounds sand

1 Measure and peg out the area required for the planter. Dig trenches for strip foundations to a depth of 10 inches; compact and level the earth.
2 Mix the concrete in a 1:4:4 cement:sand:stone ratio and place it in the trenches. Allow to set thoroughly, at least overnight.
3 Unless the structure is to be freestanding, lay the back wall as illustrated, tying in to the garden wall. The first 26 courses require seven bricks in each course. Thereafter, use a half-brick less in each of the next four courses, and reduce by a full brick in the two top courses. Cut the bricks where necessary to achieve the arched effect.
4 Allow the mortar to set thoroughly. The surrounding trim may then be laid, using bricks on edge. These will protrude at the back and front of the wall.
5 Mix mortar in a 1:4 ratio for the render and finish off the trim and front wall. Add water to what is left of the mix and smear over the back wall with burlap.
6 When all the render has set, paint the structure, then attach a gargoyle and decorative planter bowl, if desired.
7 Fill the planter with earth, and plant it out.

This sleek but simple barbecue design incorporates seating on the perimeter of a brick paved patio. Built from face-bricks, it has a sophisticated appeal which will suit the more formal garden plan. The pillar on one side may be used as a table, and there is room for storage of cordwood under the cooking surface. Although the materials specified call for a fibercement pipe to help remove smoke from the chimney, a metal pipe may be used instead.

MATERIALS

Foundation
286 pounds cement
1144 pounds sand
1144 pounds stone

Brickwork
514 bricks
50 paving bricks
385 pounds cement

187 pounds lime (optional)
34 cu. inches sand (including 14 cu inches for fill)
26 x 4½ x 3 inch concrete lintel
24 x 24 x 2 inch concrete slab
72 x 6 inch fibercement pipe

1 Measure and peg out the area where the barbecue and seating are to be located. Excavate for a 1-inch slab foundation.
2 Mix and place the concrete. Leave to set.
3 Build up the walls as illustrated, using the slab to span the lower section of the barbecue structure. Leave the core of the left-hand pillar and the area below the seating hollow, and use paving bricks for the top course of the pillar.
4 Build the lintel across the front of the base of the chimney. Set the pipe behind the front chimney wall and build it into the brickwork. Allow the mortar to set.
5 Fill the hollow areas with sand and compact. Top with paving bricks.

This lovely traditional water feature may be constructed as a freestanding structure or built into a wall. Although this one was built using precast concrete materials, the illustration will enable you to build it with bricks. As the pool must be water-proof, you should use stronger concrete and mortar mixes than those specified for ordinary garden structures. Avoid using toxic lime, especially if you plan to stock the pond with fish. You may, if you wish, incorporate corbels at the sides instead of the low side walls, and top the three-brick-high front wall with swimming-pool coping instead of a rendered lip. The wall-mounted fountain is an attractive optional feature which will add an element of movement to the pond. Any fountain-head or gargoyle may be used and this can spurt directly into the pool or into a bowl set on the lip.

MATERIALS

Foundation
825 pounds cement
1650 pounds sand
1650 pounds stone

Brickwork
570 bricks
352 pounds cement
1056 pounds sand

Render
385 pounds cement
waterproofing additive (optional)
1155 pounds sand

Fountain and accessories (optional)
Precast fountain-head or gargoyle
88 inches tubing, ½ inch in diameter
2 elbow connectors, internal
   diameter ½ inch
Submersible pump with
   72-inch water head
Outdoor cable
   and conduit

1 Measure the area required for the structure. Peg and excavate a 19-inch trench for a 1-inch foundation and two brick courses. Compact the base.
2 Mix concrete in a cement: sand: stone 1:2:2 ratio and place in the trench. Level, compact, and leave to set.
3 Build up the brick walls and side pillars according to the illustrations, using a 1:3 cement: sand mix. The first nine courses of the back wall are double courses. From the shelf upward, build a half-brick wall. If precast materials are to be used, secure them with mortar.
4 When the mortar has set, fill in the upper section of the trench with dirt.
5 Chase a channel in the wall for pipework. Chip out with a cold chisel to a depth of about 8 inches.

6 Route the cabling to the pond, either through the pond wall or over the edge. Seal with silicone if necessary. Run the cable to an outside weatherproof box and connect to the electricity supply.
7 Cut off two 4-inch lengths of tubing and join them to the longer length with elbow connectors. Push into the channel and allow to extend at either end.
8 Render the entire structure, creating lips and indentations as required.
9 Once the rendered surface has set thoroughly, attach one end of the pipe to the pump and push the other end through the hole in the fountain-head.
10 Paint several coats of rubberized bitumen or any other sealant onto the inside of the pond, following the manufacturer's instructions.
11 Paint the rest of the structure.

94 in

56 in

80 in

100 in

A charming, arched brick entrance, well within the capabilities of any competent home handyman, ties in to the boundary wall and incorporates two attractive planters. The generous proportions of the arch itself give the entrance an air of importance, suitable for both small and larger spreads. Materials specified for this structure – which could also be rendered and painted rather than built in facebrick – do not include adjacent walls. Any additional brickwork you may wish to construct can be quickly quantified from the instructions provided on pages 35–36.

MATERIALS

Foundation
154 pounds cement
616 pounds sand
616 pounds stone

Brickwork
670 bricks
495 pounds cement
247 pounds lime (optional)
1980 pounds sand

1 Peg out the foundations and dig to a depth of 10 inches. Compact and level the soil.
2 Place a few bricks at the base of the planters (see page 47.) Mix concrete in a cement: sand: stone ratio of 1:4:4 and place in the excavated trench. Allow to set partially, then remove the bricks and leave overnight.
3 Build up the walls, leaving a gap as wide as the length of a brick between the single-brick, 24-course-high back wall and the half-brick, eight-course-high front wall of the planter.
4 Build up the arch, using formwork made from chipboard and hardboard to support the brickwork.
5 Top the front of the planters with a soldier course of bricks and the back wall with a header course.

100 in

116 in

METRIC/IMPERIAL CONVERSION TABLE

To convert the measurements given in this book to metric measurements, simply divide the figure given in the text by the relevant number shown in the table alongside. Bear in mind that conversions will not necessarily work out exactly, and you will need to round the figure up or down slightly. (Do not use a combination of metric and U.S. customary measurements – for accuracy, stick to one or the other system.)

TO CONVERT	DIVIDE BY
inches to millimeters	0.0394
feet to meters	3.28
yards to meters	1.093
sq inches to sq millimeters	0.00155
sq feet to sq meters to	10.76
sq yards to sq meters	1.195
cu feet to cu meters	35.31
cu yards to cu meters	1.308
pounds to grams	0.0022
pounds to kilograms	2.2046
gallons to liters	3.785

Sources of supplies for the
Home Handyman

Home Depot, Inc.
2727 Paces Ferry Rd.
Atlanta, GA 30339
404.433.8211

Lowe's Companies, Inc.
P.O. Box 1111
North Wilkesboro, NC 28556
910.651.4000

Payless Cashways, Inc.
P.O. Box 419466
Kansas City, MO 64141
816.234.6000

HomeBase, Inc.
3345 Michelson Dr.
Irvine, CA 92715
714.442.5000

Carolina Builders Corp.
3227 Welling Ct.
Raleigh, NC 27615
919.828.7471

Menard, Inc.
4777 Menard Dr.
Eau Claire, WI 54703
715.874.5911

Wickes Lumber Co.
706.N. Deerpath Dr.
Vernon Hills, IL 60061
847.367.3400

Lanoga Corp.
P.O. Box 97040
Redmond, WA 98073
206.883.4125

Grossman's, Inc.
45 Dan Rd.
Canton, MA 02021
617.830.4000

BMC West Corp.
P.O. Box 8008
Boise, ID 83707
208.338.4300

McCoy, Corp.
P.O. Box 1028
San Marcos, TX 78667
512.353.5400

United Building Centers
P.O. Box 5550
Winona, MN 55987
507.452.2361

Pelican Companies, Inc.
P.O. Box 260001
Conway, SC 29526
803.347.4235

West Lumber Company, Inc.
5775 Glenridge Dr.
Atlanta, GA 30328
404.847.7801

Anderson Lumber Co.
P.O. Box 9459
Ogden, UT 84409
801.479.3400

Lumberman's of Washington,
Inc.
P.O. Box 3406
Olympia, WA 98503
206.456.1880

Copeland Lumber Yard, Inc.
901 NE Glisan St.
Portland, OR 97232
503.232.7181

National Home Centers, Inc.
P.O. Box 789
Springdale, AR 72765
501.756.1700

Siegle's Home and Building
Centers, Inc.
1331 Davis Rd.
Elgin, IL 60123
708.742.2000

Stambaugh-Thompson Co.
3745 Hendricks Rd.
Youngstown, OH 44515
216.792.9071

These gardens will give you
inspiration for the various
structures you might want to
erect. These are the 20 most
recommended gardens, but
there is sure to be a memorable
garden open to the public in
your home state or county.

Bellingrath Gardens
Bellingrath Road, 20 miles south
of Mobile, AL.
205.973.2217

Desert Botanical Garden
5800 East Van Buren and 6400
East McDowell Roads, 8 miles
from downtown
Phoenix, AZ
602.941.1217

Balboa Park
Laurel Street and Sixth Avenue,
San Diego, CA
619.239.0512

Golden Gate Park and Strybing
Arboretum
9th Avenue and Lincoln Way,
San Francisco, CA
415.661.1316

Huntington Botanical Gardens
1151 Oxford Road, San Marino
(Los Angeles), CA
818.449.3901

Hearst San Simeon State
Historical Monument
San Simeon, CA
805.927.4621

Filoli
Canada Road, Woodside (San
Francisco), CA
415.364.2880

Nemours Foundation
Rockland Road, off Route 141,
Wilmington, DE
303.573.3333

Dumbarton Oaks and Gardens
1703 32nd Street, Northwest,

Washington, D.C.
202.342.3290

U.S. National Arboretum
3501 New York Avenue,
Northeast, Washington, D.C.
202.475.4815

Fairchild Tropical Garden
10901 Old Cutler Road, Coral
Gables, FL
305.667.1651

Savannah Historic District
Savannah, GA
912.233.6651

Hodges Gardens
U.S. 171, 12 miles south of
Many, LA
318.586.3523

Arnold Arboretum of Harvard
Arborway, Jamaica Plains,
Boston, MA
617.524.1717

Missouri Botanical Gardens
4344 Shaw Blvd, St. Louis, MO
314.577.5100

New York Botanical Garden
Bronx Park, 1 East 200th Street,
Bronx (New York City), NY
212.220.8728

Brooklyn Botanic Garden
1000 Washington Avenue,
Brooklyn (New York City), NY
212.622.4433

Biltmore Estate and Gardens
On U.S. 25, 3 blocks nth of inter-
section with I-40, Asheville, NC
704.274.1776

Longwood Gardens
Junction of U.S. 1 and PA 52,
Kennett Square, PA
215.388.6741

Colonial Williamsburg
Williamsburg, VA
804.229.1000, Ext. 2751